The Oasis Hunter

Sandeep Dahiya

The Oasis Hunter

Preface

In an enthusiastically absurd world, why not be a peace laureate, a poet? Walking on a solitary trail, away from propagandist overtones, luminously imaginative, enjoying the regaling vocal varieties of bird songs, hewing his own convictions, reverentially visionary about the religion of love, flowing with the meticulous splurge of emotions.

A poet is a poorly clad rich man laden with inner wealth. A golden lamp in a thatched hut.

There was a time when even the brightest flicker of optimism inside him ruled out the possibility of redemption. The waves of fate spared no pains to land him at a lonely, wretched shore. It'd take loads of pain to arrive at the littlest gain. It felt like he'd just followed a futile circle—returned to his idiotic basics. A nihilistic romanticism. A shipwrecked piece at the freewill of chance, tossed by salaciously flowing freeways of stormy waves.

The storms churning in his soul make him a poet. Mystically enriched. Richly resonant with the hymns of love and peace. In tune with regaling restfulness. From his basket of agonies now he draws out ecstasies. Crossing the desert he now arrives at his oasis. He has taken long-long routes to sandy failure. Success and failure lose their meaning. The golden sands—that's his oasis. It's pure karma. He gets in splendid unison with the constructive spirit.

The poet's is a most beautiful face with the saddest expression. He is a brave chaser of the oasis. A desert traveler withstanding the prodigious kicks of fate to finally reach his oasis and lie down and rest and have prophetically enlightening dreams.

Sandeep Dahiya (Sufi), April, 2025

A joyous and lively day

The morning bright,
Hopes fully in sight,
Then a dark cloudy mass
suddenly stamped its shadowy class,
It ate the sun
with thundering chuckle and darkish pun,
A sudden spell of September rain,
The birds retreated with little grain,
It seemed it'll rain for long,
Sky's tears fell with depressive throng,
Too much rain isn't good,
All go with a sad brood,
But then the sun lifted the eastern veil,
Light flickered with a victorious feel,
The winds swept away the cloud
hanging with its dark shroud,
Dark, gray, bluish, white,
the sun emerges bright,
Quickly happens all this,
Rain-bathed trees glisten with bliss,
The birds come out with chirpy showers,
Drops glisten on flowers,
And everything is again
as it's supposed to be after a brief rain,—
a normal rain-washed day
with its sun, clouds, rains, winds,
all having an equal say,
The day accepts all,
These are all its call,
The rise and the fall,
It won't be a day
without its undulating ray,
Just like life won't be life
without its order and strife.

The witness box

When you steal
and nobody is watching,
Remember You are there
as the judge and police.

When you tell a lie,
And all believe you with an 'aye',
Remember You are there
standing mute with a cold sigh.

When you are angry at your enemy,
And find the entire blame in your foe,
Remember You are there
looking at the enemy within.

There will be a day
when this You in you
will come forward
and make you stand
in the witness box
to turn witness against yourself.

Don't meet in the court as enemies,
Meet You in you
before it's too late
and die as your own enemy.

A tiny lamp

Go to some little shrine of love
where even eagles turn dove,

And light a lamp,
Carry it to your life's camp,
Hold it
from the wind's hit,
Keep it safe, the glow,
The joyous flow,
Walk slow,
Rejoice
over this lovely choice.

The creator

Life is a throw of dice,
You have the choice
to aim, roll and throw
with all focus on your brow,
But the outcome is open
to many probabilities
beyond your control.

Then why should one throw
with so much determination
furrowed on one's brow?

One should do it,
Because if you just sit
without creating chances the least bit,
Even the probabilities will die,
Left you'll be with a cold sigh,
When you put your effort's stake
that's where all probabilities and chances
lie in a creative lake.

Your effort is the mother
of the myriads of outcomes,
They may look beyond your control,

But you're in the central role,—
the shining pole
around which creations flow
and chancy stars shine, sizzle and glow.

The winds of change

Mankind's truth
is a weathercock,
It will swing
to the direction of his
winds of desire, ambition,
greed, hate, anger,
It'll suitably point to
where it's desired.

The protagonist

There is a point
when one has to change
from a spectator to a participant,
And jump onto the stage,
Play, act and sing,
Perform one's part well.

Not that earlier was no part,
It was,
But it was too small
for a big character,—
like a spaceship
locked and docked
in its hanger on earth.

The dark-hearted torch-bearer

Sometimes misery sneaks into
such a secretive corner in us
that even we can't see it,
And thinking it to be gone,
we take a torch
and go seeking happiness outside,
But we fail,
Wherever we arrive
with our tiny puddle of light,
darkness jumps one step ahead,
keeping happiness at bay,
It'll remain so
because we carry
that bubble of misery inside us
and try to light the outside world.

Go within,
Look inwards,
Hunt that hiding darkness;
that hidden corner,
The moment
the light of your awareness
falls on it,
it vanishes,
Darkness bows out,
Then you needn't run around
to annihilate the gloom.

Gold

The weighing scale doesn't differentiate
between gold and iron,
But the human heart does,

In the human heart
a gram of gold is worth
thousands of green trees,
It's more valuable than
even many other human hearts,
The trees can be cut,
Trust broken,
Air polluted,
Earth poisoned,
And souls singed,
All this can be done
to uphold the value of gold;
to maintain its ruling crown;
its authority and superiority
over life, love and smile.

Effortless win

A screw-shaped swirl of life
taking you in its eddying grip,
The tourbillion pool of adversities,
The maelstrom ring of trap
in the stream of your life,
The ghoulish outfall,
The mouth of misery
pouting to chuck you up,
The overpowering vortex of uncontrollables
taking you in its whirlpool.

Fight it on the surface
and it'll eat your energies,
Swaying, splashing you
as you try to stay afloat,
It gets a sadistic pleasure
watching you tossed like
a twig on its eddying surface,

Don't allow yourself to be
kicked like a ball on the surface,
Cooperate with its
screwing drill into its innards,
Dive without resistance,
Its own fury is its undoing,
You go into its guts,
Your acceptance and faith
it can't digest,
Your unresisting flow
eats its stomach,
Then it spews you out
of its pointed base in the depths,
You are delivered
with your energies intact,
You are a newborn baby then,
Ready to write a new chapter.

Walking in a dark cave

There are times when
your heart gets shrunk,
wrung dry
and de-juiced by pain.
It becomes small
and darkness swallows it.
Accept it.
Fight it
and darkness becomes a demon.
Accept it.
Allow it to squeeze you more.
All this breaking
is in fact making,
It will push you
to the breaking limit,
You have to stop it

just a step before that
with your faith in life,
It'll hold you in its womb,—
in that creative pitch black cocoon,
And deliver you,
Open you again
to life, light and love.

Pain and its child—gain

Charred , shredded, scattered
pieces of love,
The heart would always retain them
and discard them not,
even if they cut and lacerate,
Because even though broken,
they still reflect its soul,
Like Phoenix they will flower,
The raging fires of hate,
anger and fears will scorch them,
But the crop of love
will rise from the ashes.

A heart would be no heart
if not for its essential core—love,
The latter might be broken
and shredded to pieces,
But it'll triumph
and rise from the fury and fire
to smile as refreshed 'love'.

Changing seasons

In the icy cold,

the frozen seed of pain,
waiting for the spring thaw,
warmer days, brighter sun.

It then blooms into love,—
a dewy fresh blossom
on a new day.

We live our life
like changing seasons:
spring's youthful love blossoms;
summer's hot sweating passion;
autumnal shedding and surrender
to the inevitable;
lying frozen in winters,
buried under icy layers of pain;
to bloom in spring again.

Defrosting

The wintertime frozen dream-self
now warms up to be an awake-self,
The icy clods melt
and the trickle of life starts,
Aha, sizzling bright February sun
going like a knife through the cold wind,—
an interplay of fire and ice,
Spring flowers taking birth
under dew-showers,
Soul brimming with joy
under clear blue sky,
Life triumphant to come abloom
after death came within an inch of life.

The illegal migrant

In tune with coquettish cooing,
you take a refreshing plunge
into the pool of love,
Excitement hooks you,
making you a not-so-elegant reveler,
But forget it not o thou journeyman
going boastfully on the path of love,
Remember that by falling in love
you have simply booked
a round-trip ticket
with an open return date,
Return you'll with a reversed fate,
It's just a stamp of limited visa
on the passport of your heart,
You'll have to come back
and squirm like an irascible caterpillar
once the adventure fever is gone.

Distances

You might be embracing someone
but still that person
might be miles away from you in heart.
And someone might be miles away
yet be there right in your heart's center.

Be a generative canvas

With its impish quirks,
the darkness that was seeking
the silvery rivulets of shape

from its shapeless mass,
Now it finds a form
in his heart.

Never forget that
even light is seeking
shape, form, embodiment,
Allow it,
Open up,
It will sneak in,
Filling you up.

Safe zones

A fish's drowning is on the land
where you stand
safe on the lovely sand,
And you drown
like a miserly pathetic clown
where she swims
with life full to the brims.

We are kings in our safe zone
but paupers around other's throne.

The song of life

A sweltering tropical night,
The electric saw of her heartlessness
cutting my dead heart's woods,
I salvage a fragment of myself
from the chopping house,
I carry the cutting like a treasure,

The melody is still alive
in its wooden fibers,
That's where my *tapasya* lies,
I've to work like a passionate artist
and shape the flute
to bring it closer to life,
Then like a flautist
touch my lips to the flute
to come still closer to life,—
to love, to hope, to smile.

Cosmic crash

Among the clatter and chatter,
Shifting specks and pulsating ripples,
Wavy swirls and mournful elegy of emotions
in the vast recesses of heart,
the generous dimensions of her presence
give me a differently abled self,
Wherein I measure my time differently,—
the heart pierced by the arrows of linear time dies
and its spirit flies in the loops of cyclical time:
the past pushing into the present;
the present barging into the future;
the future stabbing the past from behind,
It's a grand collision,
A marvelous crash.

The key

Enclosed in the fencing
of my ignorance, darkness and misery,
Standing like a poor, meek lamb,

I saw two worlds,—
a joyless *me* in the circle;
and the *other* one outside the circle,
full of lush green
and rippling streams of freedom.

The chasm between the two worlds
seemed insurmountable,
The happy *they* and the sad *me*.

I moved along the fence
trying to find a way out,
There I came across a locked gate,
The lock rusted and the key missing,
And whatever strength was left,
I used in searching for the missing key.

A folly it was,
Just like seeking a cap
that one already wears on one's head,
Because the key was always there,
Like it's with all of us,
It was there
in the safe chest of my heart,
The golden key,
The key of small love—self-love,
The key to open the box
and retrieve another key,
the key to bigger love,
to boundless freedom.

The return of the native

Yanked off the hinges,
Torn away and blown to pieces,

Buried under the rubble,
Cut off from the rays of hope,
Dark clouds of locusts
devouring the crop of my effort.

Shame-stabbed,
Pacing the room like a caged animal,
Destiny's chainsaws
cutting, clawing and gnawing
through the fibers of my existence.

Carrying autumnal colors in spring,
The serrated edges of memories
cutting the structure of my world,
The ghosts of sadness outside
always ready to barge into me.

That was how I set out
to kill the demons outside,
Went far and wide,
forgetting those that I carried
in the safe secrecy of my own self.

It was like a dust collector
carrying a huge burlap sack,
Needlessly carting dust
oblivious to gems hidden in heart.

I went too far away
from my own self,
Got lost, cried, felt orphaned,
That's when I felt Her touch,
Mother nature's brace,
The furrows on my forehead
smoothened with Her touch,
It was then a slow crawl to recovery,
I felt the chirring, buzzing mystery

of the emptiness around a rainbow.

There I stood in a wooded corner,
The time brewed a heady spirit
mixing tears and laughter,—
the potion to mend broken hearts,
The trees smiled among
the twisting vines of triumphs and travails,
Juicy, plentiful harmony pervading the air,
The birds with effervescent chorus of hope,
Each moment extending its realm of
harmony, ease, joy, lightness.

I felt in communion with vastness,
Vast stretches invaded with peace,
I was no longer a lonely lighthouse
struggling against the dark,
I felt like sun during the day
and like moon during the night.

It's very easy to fall prey to sadness
and become a rock,
But it's still easier to turn a happy soul
who chats with trees
and sings to flowers.

Far away in the solitude of a forest
I felt closer to humanity
than I ever felt even in a crowded bazaar
rubbing shoulders with human bodies,
There I was lonely, distanced,
Here I was alone
but so-so near to humanity in my heart.

Sharing the unsaid mixed in the silence,
I saw, felt, touched, tasted, heard holy scriptures
in forests, flowers, streams, blue skies, birds,

My religion became life itself,
God and godliness pervading humanly
and non-humanly on this vast canvas.

Reinvigorated, refurbished, renovated,
I then return to the busy streets,
The streets carrying the same old clatter,
But all has changed,
The shield of silence enveloped around
keeps me wired
to that far-flung harmony.

The return of the native
who is in tune with
the undertone of silence
even in a clattering bazaar.

Now I don't close my eyes
to meditate,
I open them
to see this endless magic,
this infinite beauty.

The defeated man

There stands the defeated man,
Lines of worry etched on his face,
Blizzards pelting the petals
of the flower of his fate,
The sun setting in the eyes,
The light fading out
and the night settling
as dark circles under the eyes,
Almost ground into dust by destiny,
Tension unspooling in his gut,

The ravenous flames of nightmares
chasing him even during the sunlit day.

In the pit of dark,
all he needed was her sympathy,
but never pity,
And this still surviving
streak of confidence and self-worth
seemed arrogance to her,
It opened a chasm between them,
which won't be closed by
pity or angry words
or even attempts at fake lovemaking.

Romancing with freedom

Don't make yourself small
by chasing the shadows
that were never yours,
If the shadows are all that
you can chase,
let these by your own
instead of blindly following others'
for petty gains and conveniences,
Because in chasing your own shadows,
you are still near the axis of your being
and open to redemption one fine day.

It's advisable to carry the hefty weight
of your own dead dreams
instead of floating in the
webs of others' dreams and desires,
Crawl on the ground
o thou dung beetle
instead of flying like a glowworm

in the darkness of others' hearts.

The empty canvas

Your absence
is like a vast presence;
like the sky,
Pervading and high,—
the endless canvas of one
overarching attachment
in which minor attachments,
desires and little heartbreaks
drift like tiny clouds,
The floating signs
of all lesser attachments,
They spring up,
float and drift away,
As if these are your offspring,
You the queen attachment,
The vast sky;
the great emptiness
that remains despite all attempts
to fill it with multiple rainbows.

The crippled

We have broken limbs
in our soul,
We are always looking
for a cast and sling
in the form of
special people in life,—
family, friends, lovers,

The cushion support,
The eternal need for soft bonds
to deal with stony realities.

Rebuilding and reconstruction

It's only about putting stitches
on the gaping wound;
rebuilding the broken walls;
hiding the tears behind a smile;
and trying to convince oneself
that all is well,
And keep believing in hope and life
despite the creeping shadows of
death, disorder, pain and suffering.

Change

You arrive at her door
and it's like
a fresh whiff of air,
You leave feeling
her sad sigh on your back.
Then there is a mysterious
realignment in her heart,
And neither your arrival
nor your departure
holds any significance
like it did earlier.

Smile

Her smile giving a voice
to his rainbow of emotions,
No wonder,
those were
his most lively, vibrant moments.

Wonders of heart

Heart is the master transformer,
Today it's a scented flower for someone,
But tomorrow it might be
a stone for that very same person.

The happy prisoner

Infatuation is a sweet infection,
She getting under your skin,
A sweetly itching bug,
Tingling your skin
to make you feel her presence,—
almost continuously,
The heady, rich scent of her memories
rushing in like luscious spring
after snowy, barren, frozen months.

The heart expanded with love,
Blossomed like a flower,—
an orchard where
the scented flowers of her smiles
kiss the dewy diamonds;
where the ripe fruits of her kisses

dangle with the juicy prospects of
sight, touch, taste, delicious smell.

Her absence
weighing with a heavy presence,
Her smile
spreading the message of love and beauty,
You feel walled in,
sheltered, protected, safe,
Like you are in a rock fort
in her mushy, soft, warm embrace,
Separated and segregated
from the chaos of life.

A beautiful prison
where the love-chained prisoner
becomes a canvas
for the unplanned strokes of nature,
Weaving a magic,
Painting his own lush and vibrant
image of paradise,
Shaping all pains into hope,
All this while,
her image sweetly dodging
across the chaos of his mind.

A sympathetic halt

The soul of forest goddess
trapped in the charred ruins
of a burnt forest,
Her body ravaged by
the human pride, vanity, greed, lust.

O thou lone journeyman,

Don't just go nonchalantly
through her yowling waves of pain,
Even if you can't do much,
sit among the ashes in silence,
Because even your unvoiced, kindly presence
with someone crying in pain
is a contributing factor to her healing,
Be there as a witness
to the night's gentle dewy kiss
on the ashes that were once lovely petals,
Just by doing so
you help and encourage the Phoenix spirit.

Holy nuptials

Life is reaching up to
the sun and sky,
Death is seeking rest
on the bed of mother earth,
Being is settling into
the rhythms of non-being,
While non-being strives to
get the sparkling smile of stars.

Merry ghosts

The undying fire of memories alive inside,
Smoldering with suffocating smoke,
Sometimes it flares up suddenly,
Throwing pale, flickering light,
Showing moving figures and shifting shapes
creeping like secretive nocturnal lovers,
All lanced by love,

happily melting into the folds of night
full of rolling mass of pain.

The magic wand

Love in her eyes very obvious,
The overpowering love trampling fears,
His words tingling her heart
to leave it fluttering
with a rainbow of emotions,
His touch unleashing
a galactic storm of passion
across the pores of her skin,
His embrace gathering her
and rooting her into sweet belongingness,
His walk with her
setting a course for a lovely destination,
His look at her
blooming a smile on her lips,
His presence enabling her to flow
into the emptiness in him
and acquire a shape
that fulfills his own form.

Blooming

Whenever we
misbehave with someone,
we are merely trying to
squelch our bitterness,
Whenever we
pour hate on someone,
we are just throwing sand

on the fire of self-loath,
But when we love someone,
we are uncovering ourselves;
opening a window into our being
for the sunlight to barge in
and flood us with joy and healing,
We open up and receive the grace,
just like a bud opens to be a flower
to be kissed by sunlight and bees.

Rebellion

My feelings molded by social rules,
I dived pretty deep
but still missed her full depth,
Tamed by social trimmings,
my young self represented the old,
But I'd revolt sometime
and the old would represent the young,
A *sirsasana* for the spirit it would be.

The pirates of love

Everyone thinks
love is for him or her,
But it is not,
It isn't for everyone,
To most of us,
its fake, pirated copy would fit,—
a poor quality imitation;
just enough to give us
a false sense of comfort and security.

Real love is intense,
It's a storm,
I don't think most of us
can bear its naked authenticity,
It burns, singes, hurts, peels,
robs us of the fake sense of comfort,
plunders hypocrisies,
strips us naked to face our frailties,
It has very sharp edges
in its original version,
No wonder
the majority buys the fake copy,
Just like the essence of honey
mixed in a drum of plain sugar.

The lost diamond

The flames of her passion
trying to lick guilt and shame
from my face,
Screaming out her love,
Pouring out her entire essence
from her lovely soul.

Whose fault it was?
Did I simply allow her
to slip out of my loop?
Did I simply let her drift away?
Did I put enough effort to retain her?

Maybe I failed,
Probably I'd have still failed
had I given all
and she would've succeeded,
For love can never be forced,

It drops like a ripe fruit
after a time,
I know this,
Still I mourn the loss of that kiss,
For it's human to feel the pain
born of losing the things
that we suppose we own.

Rebirth

Facing the wildfires of life,
Walking through the soot,
leaving black footprints
on the ashen floor,
Darkness swelling inside,
widening the gulf between
dreams and reality,
Weariness pouring out of eyes,
Carrying the look and feel
of a wounded animal,
Billowing black-blue waves of pain
dragging their sharp prongs
through the heart
to dredge sorrows
perfumed with sweetness.

Blackened snowflakes
slicing through the softest parts.

Don't wither completely, I tell myself,
Fragment thyself, make chambers,
So that even if you die in one part,
you may start growing in some other,
where anger will soften into acceptance,
leaving you hopeful enough

to see the miracle of sunshine
on a freezing, stormy day.

Evolution

Rewiring myself to see
the beauty of wild flowers,
acknowledge the gentle welcome of trees,
hear the friendly whisper of breeze,
enjoy the songs of birds,
listen the holy whispers of love
cutting through unholy noise.

Overhauling my material existence
to make it sublime and pure like soul,
To serve as a link between earth and sky,
Bending towards light
with a promise of love.

Truth, the enemy

Truth covered under nice manners,
polite gestures, benevolent expressions,
fine clothing, intellectual bearing,
shiny eyes and attractive smiles,—
the worldly tools
covering a grave vulgarity: the naked truth.

For all our varnished hypocrisies
and polished make-believe demeanor,
truth must be uncouth, raw, even vulgar
in its original, pure form,
That's why it's repressed, condemned,

martyred, bled to death,
It's after all
the common enemy
of the collective falsehood and fakery.

The palace pauper

Her warm, embracing presence,
An entire sea of excitement
surging through her,
Her body decorated with joy,
Skin's electricity-charged pores,—
a living palace,
And there I walked
bored, lonely and afraid
to feel safe, loved and cared.

The fire

The fire that ate peace,
It chucked out many rarities:
an old tree with a new nest;
a handwritten manuscript
without another copy;
the sole manuscript of an ancient book;
the wood that was charred
without manifesting
what was hidden inside,—
the beautiful statue;
the heart that got singed
and the canvas burnt;
the smile slaughtered
on innocent lips

that would have blossomed
a nobler, kinder place.

The fire going into the eyes,
blinding and burning the dreams,
The fire parching the flesh
and singing the soul,
The fire in our minds
smoldering forever
to burn the paradise
that was offered to us
by the lovely, smiling,
benevolent mother nature.

The creeper

Feelings entwining,
Mingling,
Twisting around each other,
Holding out tendrils like creepers,
Grasping each other's soft stalks
like vines to soar higher.

To merge,
To seep,
To crash into each other
like sea waves on a beach.

Flowing together
to become something nobler;
to feel one's presence
through the other.

The tired tailor

The tired tailor,
Working on a short man's coat
stolen by a tall man,
Laboring to make it fit the thief.

The tired tailor,
Working to mend a thin man's coat
falling in the hands of a fat man,
Striving to cover naked corpulence
with little strip of cloth.

God the struggling tailor,
Fixing the misfits,
A tired and worn out tailor!

The robbers

Those who can't create,
they believe in destruction,
They don't do much,
They create destruction at the most,
They rob others
of their rights to creativity.

The shop of love

Love at the spectrum's lower end
would need something in return,—
a sweet-sour worldly barter,
But it's still love,
the base model though.

Love at the spectrum's upper end
would want nothing in return,
It just is,
Just selfless giving,—
the top model;
pristine, pure, pricey.

Woman

You have already paid a big price
by being a woman
in a male-dominated world,
You then accept your status
of being under debt forever,
So you keep repaying your debts
in bits and pieces
on a daily basis
till your last breath.

Love

Love is solid in the bones;
fluid in blood;
airy fresh in breath;
tingling in touch on the skin;
sweet in smile on the lips;
tasty in words on the tongue;
light and hope in the eyes;
and lots of flowers
in the garden of heart.

The pathless path

Creating a path to God,
Flying like a bird
facing no barriers of boundaries,
brawls, rituals, sectarianism,—
the pathless path,
The path always there
but not visible
till you move on it,
Like the path in the air
that was always there
but didn't manifest
till some bird
took a joyful sortie
in its airy swirls.

A fresh dose of joy

Fresh winds enlivened the spirit,
Cut through timidity
with the knife of loving familiarity
and friendliness,—
a growing closeness
embracing with a kiss.

Is it bodily attraction,
or pleasant feeling of proximity,
or being relaxed in her presence,
or synchronization of thoughts,
or sweet melding of emotions,
or vibes on the same frequency?

The priests of imprisonment

God is like the warden
whom we try to bribe
to get into the prison cells
to meet our acquaintances,
family and friends,—
money, power, health, prestige, name, fame.

And our fears are the priests,
the lesser gods
manning the doors and wired fences,
We have to placate them too
with obeisance, offerings and rituals.

The smoker of memories

Passing through the darkness
of the long corridor
smelling of past memories,
Feeling destiny's roughly hewn walls,
Eyes speaking of pain,
There I walk with my once golden self
turned into crumbling chalk.

The gently sculpted folds of your love
turned to sharp, cutting edges;
the lovely embroidery and beadwork
turned a rough, barren terrain,
Taking a long drag of smoky memories
from the flaming cigarette of the past,
I cough
and realize
love is rarely enough.

The fallen artist

Bright, unrealistic colors of love,
Childish, whimsical, even idiosyncratic,
Painting an alternate reality;
a different dimension of life
on the plain, routine canvas,
We use cheap paints and crude brushes
to shape something
to go along our dreams,—
a concrete solidified dream
in an ephemeral world,
Drawing the outlines of hope, safety, light.

Then you realize,
it doesn't meet your expectations,
So you pick up a soapy mop
to erase the once lovely painting,
which turned into a comic-tragic graffiti,
You become a cleaner
from an artist that you were before.

From fine lines to sloppy mop,
Flop!
Why?
Because we have needs
in different compartments,
One picture centered around one object
doesn't go into different chambers:
emotions, thoughts, dreams, desires, lust, needs.

The brush of love
temporarily appears to wade
through all these different needs,
We believe it's giving all that we need,
Soon we realize it doesn't,
The picture disappoints us,

We then just stay with each other,
Trying to believe that
we have happily been together.

The dark which is brighter than the light

There is a type of darkness
that feels one with fear;
the visible manmade threats,
actions born of hate, greed
and our own suspicions.

Then there is another darkness
that envelops you with friendly embrace,
An invisible representative of all that
which makes you feel good in life.

Through darkness I walk by choice,
outweighing the former by the latter,
Darkness is a sieve,
It allows you to segregate good from bad,
I try to cast away the little stones
left above the wire mesh
and let in the fine sand of joy and goodness
trickle into the bowl of my heart.

Don't underestimate darkness,
If you learn to hold
all that which makes you feel good
then it enables you to see
even clearer than the daylight.

Becoming a bigger entity

The trees are very kind,
Soak their kindness,
Accept the sweetness of fruits,
the scent of flowers,
the freshness of air,
the beauty of bright dewy mornings.
We are here
to fulfill mother nature's purpose
by being loving, kind and receptive
to all her smiles and charms,
We do that by
welcoming and feeling that happiness
that oozes from her in pristine forests,
That's what mother nature wants from us,
And a bit of furthering the same
from our end if we shall.

The core of pain in the bubble of gain

So much darkness
under the sunny façade of a bright noon,
So many vulgarities
hidden beneath polished etiquettes,
So much pain and suffering
stocked under confident, smiling faces,
So much hate hidden in seemingly kind hearts,
Funeral songs lurking below gay festivities,
So much pain swallowed by bright eyes,
A kind of grey darkness from inside
flushing something to the surface
that we call good, hope, joy, happiness, lawful
and socially clean as it should be.

A gentle sadhna

You have to open your heart
very-very wide to allow
the light of truth sneak in;
the music of divinity pour in;
the fresh spring air of the new reality
blossom up fully in you.

To allow this evolution,
you don't have to break mountains,
All that's needed is to be
open-doored and open-hearted.

Breakable hearts

Sometimes love has to act
outside the boundaries of social law,—
the sharply calculating basis
of the customized decree,
And gift oneself
the unique commandment;
allowing oneself just pure love,—
awakening into a new self,
an uncustomized, exclusive existence.

Not all hearts are breakable;
only some are,
The unbreakable hearts are the stony forts
for safekeeping falsehood
and debilitating conventions,
It's the breakable hearts
that have the fluidity and mellowness
to seep and creep
out of the curtailing maze

and give you
the gift of a distinctive being
in a fresh, unused cast.

Love-tangled beings

Sharing love is like sharing roots,—
groping around;
entwining to seek soul's nourishment
from connections and relationships,
The fine web of existence,
intermingling destinies:
the meeting bodies being the earth;
love the web of their entangled roots;
and their souls are the nourished ones.

Counterbalanced being

With black and white in the head
and a rainbow in the heart,
Weighed down by hate
and uplifted by love,
I feel neither vertical
nor horizontal,
It feels like
being in a different plain.

Enchained sovereigns

We are imprisoned and enchained
in our own freedoms,

Despite their appearance to bestow liberty,
that which we
take to be the proofs of free will
are in fact the bars and barbed fences,
These stop us from reaching beyond
what we have so far considered
to be the pinnacle of freedoms.

The mirror of love

The shine, light and glow from within
peeping through her eyes,
Raising inspiration
to fulfill my dreams,
With fullness of desire in my chest,
if I don't love myself,
who else will love me?
And if not now, then when?

In disharmony with nature

A see-saw of emotions
ripping through wooden fibers,
Cutting the dead wood of memories
in the heart to make
wooden dolls, statues, mannequins,
That's how most of us are:
much less alive than trees and flowers.

Customized by conventions;
wind-tangled by circumstances;
breeze-tousled by situations;
pain and suffering sculpting our destinies,

We allow ourselves to be molded
by the forces of atrophy
manifesting in our thoughts,
While the trees and even animals
seem to absorb more automatic order
into their existence,
They do it just by
allowing the open forces of nature
to shape them in harmony with eternal laws,
While we filter too much negatives and chaos
using our brainy check-dam effort
and channelize the intellectual sludge
for war, violence and strife.

A wealthy corpse

The tattoo maker
working with quiet persistence,
Tattooed a label on the heart,
which turned a quagmire,
a trapping swamp.

Life then became a mere
undoing operation managed by death
to relieve the struggler of his pain
and carry him home
as a very rich man,
who returns with all treasures
unspent during the journey.

He died very rich,
For he still possessed
all that he was born with,
He now lay like a foolish farmer
who kept all his seeds

safely hidden in his barn,
Never took them to the fields,
Never opened them to the sun's smile
and mother earth's nourishment,
In musty darkness they rot now,
Life seeped out,
Hopes and possibilities bleached,
And gloom settles on the corpse
like crows crunching a dry carrion.

It was a life unspent,
Just like a tiny rodent
merely crawled on a plywood sheet,
while wasted were the seeds
that would've made him an elephant
joyfully stomping on solid earth.

The lost traveler

Mud-caked with dark memories,
Ashen and terrified,
The serpent of shame
slithering over his heart,
Raking the dead leaves of autumn
for a rustle or murmur of life,—
the pale, crumbling leaves
that had once a lively luxuriance,
Alas, the spring was wasted,
The bus was missed,
Now the sulking journeyman
looking for some traces of life in a grave.

The predatory software

The awkward familiarity of love
tugging at your bruised self
with delicate deference,
Ripe, tender, luscious love
pouring its spicy excitement
into the bland, spoiled dish
prepared with the recipe of the broken heart,
The fresh ingredients of new love
trying to undo its own raspy touch
clawed on the heart in its previous version;
trying to wipe the melancholy
carved on the heart;
trying to put light in the eyes
where its last version settled deep sorrows;
trying to put balm on the bleeding wounds
as the prongs of past go dredging
the memories of the old version.

When was the hardware (body) sensible?
Especially when love (the software)
has this terrible urge for updation!

The oasis hunter

She burrowing a hole into his heart,
Drilling through various crusty layers of
anger, fear, guilt, insecurity and shame,
Diligently boring to reach the core,
the chamber of love
lying buried under uncouth layers.

The lovely well-digger,
Soaked with sweating love,

Working to reach the sap of love,—
the nectar of springs.

A hopeful journeywoman
seeking an oasis in the desert,
To make him feel
that he has love at his core,
not hate and animosity.

The lighthouse

Everything is meaningless
without loving and being loved,
After all, we are mere fishes
lost in the sea's vast expanses,
We are scared of getting lost
in the looming prospects of freedom
swarming its massive gloomy depths,
So we're running around
to be gaffed by the spear of love;
to be netted in love.

Aha, the sweet anarchy of love!
Love fragile like porcelain,
but still a beacon of hope,
Shining like a lighthouse
on a rocky, stormy shore,
Spreading its guiding light
among dark, choppy waters,
Fighting the muscles and tissues of darkness
just with its fragrant, lightening presence.

Love with its ephemeral intensity
sizzles across the folds of eternal apathy,
It shimmers like a lighted powdery

splash of disarming mystery,—
a sparkling kiss of life
on the embracing gentleness of death.

The guide

Unconcerned about others' judgments,
it's your right to take steps to freedom,
But remember this o thou journeyman
that one's soul should stay open to self-judgment
because that'll guide you on the path,
That'll be your key
to the channelization of your free choice
towards the best instead of the worst.

The tyrant

Love barging into the heart,
breaking all defensive barriers,
occupying the fort,
gloating on the throne,
giving orders like a triumphant autocrat.

Then its soldiers creeping up the chest
to fight the opposing armies in the throat,
The battles in the narrow pass,
Defeating the vocal cords,
Disarming them
and ordering them
to sing the sovereign's songs.

Love has to acquire all,
Its rampant armies

have to march still onwards
to twist the lips to make them
casting molds for its signature banners;
to paint the cheeks with its trademark blush;
to pour possessive light in the eyes;
to put filters in the ears
so that they hear only its eulogy songs.

Finally the marching army
creeps into the head
to win the final frontier;
to beat down the strains of reasoning,—
the last rebellious regiment.

Love wages an all-conquering war
to change everything
as per its whims and fancies,
What a sweet tyrant!
What a stern dictator!

The beauty of an imperfect world

It's a broken world
but still it has enough beauty
in its fragments
to help us hold onto
our dreams and imaginations.

It's enough to give us:
a hope to put things together;
an invitation to move on the journey;
to see the sunshine in a dewdrop;
to absorb the nourishment of life from a smile;
to feel kindness in a tear;
to see flying rainbows

on the wings of butterflies;
to hear divine melody in a hill stream;
to hear paradisiacal songs in chirping birds;
to feel and understand that
life sprouts on the edges of broken dead pieces
like wild mushrooms on dead wood.

Silence

Unspoken words
sometimes open up a chasm,
which no pearly string of words
can cover with a bridge,
And to know each other well,
we have to learn
the language of silence
emanating from someone's
walk, frown, smile or stony look.

Drowning

Life is merely a flow:
molten agonies;
floating joy;
streaming desires;
steaming passion;
evaporating dreams;
undying aspirations.

We try to cross it,
Taking it to be
the aim and purpose of life,
But the moment we reach the bank,

panting like a dog,
we turn our head
and look at the aims and goals
on the other bank,
We feel we have lost something
very important over there.

So we swim back,
And over and over again,
We get conditioned to think that
crossing the river back and forth
is the aim of life,
the proof of success,
Little do we realize that
it was supposed to be a journey,
a flow with the stream.

Mostly we realize it too late,
We don't have even that much patience
as it needs to stay joyfully afloat
in a gently flowing stream,
Fatigued with incessant crossings,
we panic and drown in the stream
just near the point
of our futile back and forth fording,
We miss the flow,
We miss all that life had to offer
on its journey ahead.

Emptying the bins

We are too crowded inside;
too full,
We need emptying,
Not by dumping the extras;

not by outright discarding
the already crammed, clogged garbage bins,
but by spreading in nature's open arms,
We just need to be in an open space
to allow 'emptying' start naturally.

The romancer of mirages

I see a huge wave of sadness
building up on the horizon,
I'm a tiny assemblage
drifting along a gentle stream in the sea,—
some pieces of junk and a bit of driftwood;
a chance assemblage by circumstantial winds,
Then a massive wave comes crashing
and tosses me ashore.

Now I'm more fragmented,—
pieces of junk here;
bits of driftwood there,
My sense of identity further broken,
With pain and jealousy,
my shattered pieces gloat over
the peaceful happy world over there,
Little do I realize that
only a fragment
sees the mirage of perfection.

The subjected ruler

Most of us are prisoners of thoughts,
How we wish to escape
the prison of our minds!

We are hostages taken by emotions,
How we wish to free ourselves
from the ensnaring swamps of the heart!
Helpless, we try to bribe for our release,
We are actually like a jailor
who feels imprisoned
in the jail he rules over.

Blunting the edges

One cannot undo
the prongs of pain and agony
by putting pleasure and luxury
on the sharp points,
You can't cover a *trishula's* sharp edges,
We keep them sharp if we do so,
But there is a technique
that can dismantle these
piercing prongs of pain,
It's the rust of indifference,
Apathy to pleasure and luxury
would naturally rust and blunt
the edges of pain.

The death of a pack mule

We never forget,
Maybe we never forgive,
or get forgiven,
Be it hate or hate(s),
or love or love(s),
We carry their bittersweet,
poignant, tart, soothing, disturbing,

happy, sad, hopeful, depressive
imprint on our skin;
their stamp on our soul;
their mark on our existence.

Some sudden dusty autumnal gust of wind
lays bare the moth-eaten, moldy
crumbling lid of the trunk of memories,
We open the lid
with gingerly fingers,
We want and don't want,
but still we do,
And from the damp, stale air inside,
with closed eyes we have our rosy smell,—
that touch, that walk together,
that kiss on the lips of that special someone,
or the pangs of jealousy, hate, anger
for those who stabbed us in animosity.

We carry the past buried in us,
in our cremation ground,—
private and personal,
And we silently visit it
to exhume golden sunshine sometime
or swamps of darkness the other time,
And then on some fine or not so fine day,
we drop like a ripe leaf
and get buried in the same graveyard.

The semi-free prisoner

A part of me is confined and chained,
Anchoring me, holding me
in a tiny, isolated bay,
In the little pool lies my hope,

On the little uninhabited island
lie my dreams, aspirations and fears.

There is a transparent wall around me,—
almost a glass wall,
And a part of me lies outside
unchained, unchecked, unconditioned,
free to roam
among the endless waves,
It comes harking,
riding the crest of waves,
yelling, surfing, enjoying
and crashes against the transparent wall.

The little pool of conditioned water
inside the atoll
gets ripples in response,
It rises and heaves a little,
Shoves against the wall
from inside the atoll.

It's a deaf conversation,
Wordless but full of gestures,
It seems like
freedom wants to be chained,
And the prisoner wants to be free.

The other side of me
enjoying this side of me,
Both eyeing each other,
Giving covetous looks,
That's how I live,—
a part of me free;
a part of me chained.

God's tiny bowl

There is a part in me
that is empty,—
a hole, a pit,
It's full of invisible pain, grief
and the shadows of lost love,
Disappointments, broken dreams
and sharp shards of memories
haunt the gloomy crater,
But it's full of something else also,—
an urge, a force, a pull,
Like a magnet,
it sucks hope, belief and faith,
These are its little sunrays
to sustain its shadows, its shades
floating like dust motes in a sunbeam.

All of us have our holes,
our emptiness full of shadows,
But that's our creative emptiness,
the genesis of our urge
to be something more.

We are God's tiny bowls,
which He playfully tries to fill
in varying colors, shapes, cuisines
to muse over His own manifestation.

The haunted, hunted species

Walking on powdery sand
hiding many corpses
under its crumbling crust,
Saving the feet from coils of barbed wire,

Afraid of rifles
peeking from behind the sandbags,
Surrounded by countless bullet scars
on the walls,
Stared at by the corpses
of once lively houses and shops,
We walk in the bloodied maze of life.

We are a very scared, insecure species,
So to feel our fears with more depth,
the war zones we have to create,—
this vast scary game of violence and anger.

We carry immeasurable inherited sorrow,
The entire species dabbed with
the clammy colors of grief,
Plastic smiles we carry at the most,
And even this vanishes
just with the clicking latch on a
creaky door with complaining hinges,—
a trigger, a fuse for blasting the fears in us,
Ribbed and ridiculed
by the captivating madness,
we carry our cranky self
on the thin paths leading to
wars, strife, violence, blood and gore.

Tyranny with life

We have limited
the idea of happiness and success
to a very few narrow paths,
Walking on these thin trajectories
some people become so inactive with life,
So much musty

in the staid, stale monotones
of what they do as a routine
without feeling any joy,
So much demure with life
that even dying seems an activity,
This is like death's petty
household tyranny with life.

The stillborn

What follows a revolution
is even worse than before,
Because it stands on too much
blood, gore and violence
within a short time,
It's a nasty kick on a pregnant belly,
Forcing a bloodied miscarriage,
It's an immature strike
leading to a premature stillborn child,
If not for the violent kick,
there would have been a healthy baby,—
a mature delivery
at an appropriate time.

Salted wounds

Drift ice floating in coastal waters,
The wounds getting salted,
And iciness (hope)
clinging like a leech,
sucking the frozen blood of effort
to remain ice,
Everything is caught

in the intersecting zone of
being and nonbeing.

The dreamer of love

I bear no concrete illusion
of being separated from the surroundings,
Yes, it exists,
but just like a passing cloud,—
a wispy shadow
scattering feeble fencing now and then,
which temporarily
shuts me off in my ego chamber,
But soon the clouds of ego pass,
The sun of unity shines,
casting away all separating shadows,
That's when I feel like
I can fly without wings
and share my 'being' with the birds,
That's when I can flow
with the fluid essence of streams;
can kiss the sky with lofty mountain peaks;
can rest like a turquoise calm lake;
can spread myself to infinity with stars,
And when I'm such,
I can easily meet you in dreams
and whisper solace and succor in your ears
on lonely nights
when you fall asleep with a sad heart,
My words will get a smile on your lips,
And I'll watch it as my own smile.

Holy whispers

I'll whisper
loving words
in your dreams
when you feel lonely.

The solitary walker

There are people who shout
and grab the most in a stampede,
There are some more who just whisper
and get onto the sidelines
to pick up what lies uncontested,
Out of these sideliners,
there are still fewer
who come out of the main-street throng
to take an abandoned empty little side alley,
With some occasional whisper
they pick up only what seems unworthy
to anyone on the main street,
Out of these latter,
a rare soul comes out of all congestion
to walk on a solitary trail
where the soul sings in freedom.

The bridge

A bit happy for what has been spared,
Carrying lots of pain
about what has been taken away,
Trudging the bridge between
happiness and sadness,

there I walk from this end to that,
unable to ensure
which side to cross over finally.

The swinging suspension bridge
seems an end in itself
rather than the means for a cross over,
The bridge made of:
gratitude, guilt, anger, pain,
relief, safety, insecurity.

The swinging bridge
swaying over the vast chasm
that life seems from it,
On it most of us walk
interminably from this side to that,
taking it to be the only journey possible,
Foolishly ignorant of the fact
that it was a mere means for crossing,—
a humble convenience or utility.

Netted butterflies

Melting with delight,
Tickled by the blush of youth,
The air sweet with wildflower scent,
Adolescence rushing to the peak
to quench the thirst of all curiosities,
And awaits there
the trapper of butterflies—love,
With its beautifully designed, silky net,
To catch lovely colors on the wings,
To see them flapping
for the agony and ecstasy of
loving and being loved.

What else are we when in love,
if not netted butterflies?
We love getting netted
in the silk threads
of that sweet bondage,
We just pine to be caught
by emotions all fiery and hot,
Aah, the cupid's high scoring, slaying shot!
❁

Self-charity

Be a stony support to someone
and that person naturally becomes
a velvety cushion support to you,
Because when you give support,
you receive the same as well,
A kindly giving
is a subtle taking in a nobler form,
Giving a hand to the fallen
is a loving means to
avoid falling yourself,
Words of sympathy for someone
are a prayer for your own benefit,
To be there for someone in need
is to invest in your own safety
against similar challenges in your journey,
Good or bad,
what we do to others
is primarily looping back to us
in the same form without camouflage.

In the same vein,
being friendly to a lovely soul
is to befriend one's best version.

Welcoming the self into a cage

The immensity of the free skies,
its vastness,
its endless vistas of freedom
get us scared,
We soak in the freedom initially,
Then we fear we'll be lost,
We feel lonely in the free enormity,
The adventure dies,
Pursued by our own fears,
we rush into a cage,
Its known confines
guarding us against the unknown,
We drop the anchor,
We get chained
to a smile, a kiss, an embrace,—
a sweet entanglement;
a pleasant bondage called 'love'.

Bulldozer scrunching over soft buds

You meant it to be the past,
It's not supposed to
collide with my present,
The crunching tyres
of the big armored vehicle
(raising sands of guilt, anger and embarrassment)
shouldn't ram into my present's lurching cart,
But they do,
Seems like you remotely
operate this rampager

to take further revenge
and turn the present into
a grotesque wreckage.

The rusted padlock

The heavy, rusted padlock,
Its key missing,
Hanging on an old massive door
of a dark chamber,
Hiding an ever-shut, secretive vault,
Spooky.

Once it was a golden kiss-lock,
Would snap open with the spring,
Would snap down
and close upon the previous season.

And before that
it was all open,
No lock,
Just an open secret of love.

Eclipse on the path

Love holds you in a firm grasp;
in tight fist,
Entwining your destinies
for a paired chemistry,
That intimacy, familiarity, closeness,
The shared identity;
the overlapping zone,
Two molten selves

lovingly creeping into each other,
Sweet superimposition,
Tingling eclipsing of one by the other,—
alternating eclipses,
He covering her
and she him.

But very rarely we are
two bodies moving in the same direction,
Like celestial bodies,
we cross paths from different directions,
Eclipse and pass across each other,
Then we drift away,
The shared zone keeps decreasing,
Moving away like strangers,
As if there was no acquaintance,—
a build-up of eternal estrangement.

Walking in the love-lane

The sweeping love-spools,
almost to the extent of being crazy,
A rush of positive chemicals they say,
But what a powerful natural intoxication!
The days get colored in new light,
You feel more alive than you remember,
A convalescence from past pains,
A reimbursement for the losses,
An empowerment against all maladies,
You feel lucky
to sleep-walk in the love-lane,
It helps you dreamily float
above and beyond
the concrete puzzles of life.

Betrayal

Why couldn't I love you enough
to keep the joy that you once felt
on my touch?
Why couldn't I keep
that shine in your eyes,
which sparkled at my sight?
Why couldn't I keep
your dream in being love going
as you walked, talked in daylight?
Why couldn't I keep nourishing
that smile on your lips in my company?
The failure to do so
is maybe a betrayal,
It's better to accept one's failure,
It clears at least one dark spot
from your conscience,
And in doing so,
you let her go
with her reputation intact,
In any case, you are sad,
Adding culpability to it
would lessen bitterness, I think.

A journey through time

Past and future
are parasitic in temperament,
Always seek to expand, grow and stretch
beyond reality,
beyond practical limits.

The poor 'present' is a casualty,

It's like a pointed peak,—
small but high, lofty, uplifting
where the upslope of future
and the down-slope of past meet,
intersect and forget their tension momentarily,
And that's when we actually live.

In childhood, we've more of 'present'
and hence we're lively,
The youth is a run for the future,
As we walk, we leave behind a trail
and future shrinks,
past stretches,
There comes a point
when all we've is the 'past'
in our old bones, dimmed eyes,
Again we arrive
at a phase of dulled, dimmed present,
Just a grave to look forward to;
few surviving memories
in the tiny vanishing puddle of life,
mired in mud,—
a few fishes flapping sometimes,
The past meaningless
and the present
almost a curiosity about death.

The scrap yard of love

That's how I gathered her,—
a sad pile of
shards, fragments, broken pieces,
But that's love,
Broken pieces feel like
soft rosebuds in your arms,

They bleed the skin
as you press with gentle warmth,
You become a maker or mender,
The broken pieces get together
and acquire a shape in the kiln
of your care and share,—
a lovely woman in your arms,
full of dreams and desires;
strong, confident, vigorous.

Love first softly brushes,
then sadistically crushes,
Now it's your turn to be broken
and spill out of her arms,
Get shattered and scattered,
Waiting for some enchanting
treasure hunter of love
to see the potential in the broken pieces,
To gather you up;
your fragments in her lovely arms,
Love will sprout again,
Giving you a new shape
in new arms with fresh charms.

The fungus on the self

If you allow loneliness to push you,
it'll gorge on your choices and confidence,
It'll corner you like a little mouse
shivering with fear,
seeing snakes and cats
in all that which moves around.

Loneliness is the crazy lover,
It'll pursue one, always,

That's its nature,
Whom does it catch?
The one who can't outpace it,
Who are its prey?
The ones heavily burdened,—
with guilt and anger of the past;
or foolish illusions of the future.

Beat it, outpace it, confidently,
Like unburdened, swift horses,
Light like wind,
Swift like arrows,
Clanking their hooves on the cobblestones,
Pacing to the tunes of the present,—
Now,
Not an alley, side street or crossing
misses their confident eye,
They make choices,
They are self-assured,
Loneliness lags far behind them,
The bulb of their presence
dispels the darkness
where the night-bugs of loneliness
sprout like poisonous fungus.

Strangers

Little instruments of intimacy
in the vast machine of love,
Enjoying the soft brush of lips,—
a solid stone fort's support;
a steely assurance,
Melting into each other,
Skins seeping into each other,
Leaving no further distance to be covered,

Making a single entity
in thoughts, feelings and actions.

Then the walls crept between them,
Big stony walls,
Intimidating blocks
separating them,
Dividing them,
Cutting them apart,
The jarring fissures,
The glue-work of abandoned love
seeping and cementing the walls,
The walls crept high enough
to leave them complete strangers.

They carried each other's torn skin flakes
on their changed identities,
The dead flakes of martyred love
sticking as sweet-bitter memories.

They walked along the stony walls,
There are no doors or windows,
Nostalgic entreaties fail,
Hope is lost,
They know that
both of them died in their own ways,
Losing a part of the self
in losing the other,
Thus they moved ahead wounded,
Then drifted away even from the wall.

A good human being

A collector of broken things,
An assembler of discarded pieces,

Making it a better world
without setting it as a goal;
just by being selflessly kind;
just a safe, secure bubble of existence;
being loving where
the outside strife won't break in;
sometimes even giving shelter
to the people who shun love
purely due to the
fear of losing a loved one.

Belittling bestiality

What is the purpose of attaining freedom,
if you stay locked up inside yourself?
What purpose your wings serve,
if you decide to stay in the
cage of dogmas, curtailing conventions
and belittling beliefs forged by others?
What purpose your mind serves,
if it's fogged with the clouds of
others' hate, greed and ambitions?
What purpose your legs serve,
if they merely follow the mass
sleepwalking after a hypnotizing manipulator?
What purpose your hands serve,
if they are mere instruments
to fulfill someone's evil designs?
What purpose your eyes serve,
if you see just the craftily managed
scenes to pamper the *little man* in you?
What purpose your ears serve,
If they just drum to the beats of
jingoism, rhetoric and false narratives?

If you are such a person as above,
you die as a baby even in old age
because you left your potential untapped;
almost untouched and virginal,
Born as a baby and dead as a baby,
Where was life during those long decades?

Warring with the self

I was sufficient already,
But then I began to see myself
through others' eyes,
And my sufficiency crashed,
Something missing in this,
Something in that,
Sadly brooding I sat,
Pampered by fate
as its pessimistic, sulking pet.

Long before others,
we judge our own self,
Our own critical eye
cuts, bruises, lacerates, downplays,
devaluates and thumbs us down,
Showing us in poor light,
Long before the outsiders' shears
prune our self-specific, luxuriant sprawl,
we give self-inflicted wounds to our own self,
And around these home-made wounds,
we keep building defensive ramparts,
Whereupon we stand like a hound
and throw catapults
at the imagined enemies around.

The stamp of love

We will recover from hate
but never from love
if it has gone wrong,
Brightest smiles have the potential
to sire bitterest tears,
Lovely sweetness can easily
change to ugly sourness,
Petals hide thorns.

In love we are
on the edge of a precipice,
That's why it's exciting
and not boring like
the plateau of other common emotions,
We are at a titillating height
and feel floating over the lower terrain,
But we are on the edge,
On an edgy adventure of
body, mind and soul,
Mostly we fall into the pit,
Dump or get dumped
into the heap of pain,
Then we see some lovely new face
peering over the edge,
And again we crawl up,
holding the rope of hope.

One may climb as many times
as one can manage
but the bruises of at least one fall
remain there forever on our flesh,
However hard one tries to heal it
with the ointment of fresh loves,
the scar but remains
with its peculiar purple leering smile.

The master juggler

Memories are trapped in soul
because time is circular,
It spins, circles
and creates a web;
a cage around our being,
It has a fine thread
to weave its maze,—
past, present and future,
Like a master performer,
it juggles these three balls,
Keeps them in the play
in its two hands:
the known and the unknown;
fear and safety;
life and death.

Past, present and future
keep searing through us
at their own free will,
No wonder, we live life
in mere fragments,—
hope-despair, love-hate,
dreams-reality, tears-smiles.

We are fragments,
And we flow for
completion, contentment and rest,
Like water running
from the hills to the sea,
We are imperfections
seeking perfection,
Pushing, colliding, mixing,

adding, subtracting,—
the mathematics of life
to solve the puzzle of our existence;
to give it a purpose, a solution.

Time meanwhile nullifies all equations,
The biggest equation summing to zero,
The kings vanish,
The dictators mingle to dust,
The castles turn to leveled ground,
All fractions (big and small)
fly and then hit the bottom
and get mixed in the same soil,
Only time remains,
It chuckles in its totality
from among the cosmic web.

Sweet melancholy of love

I'm watching your waves
flooding, crashing, smashing
in my being.

I'm watching the storm
in the desolate desert,
The sand flying,
Burying one truth,
Shape it into something different
with new ribs,
Only to bury it again,—
the creative whirlpool
in the womb of your soul,
The fierce incubation.

The traveler moving to

reach a subtle treasure,
unbothered of worldly losses,
I'm witnessing her journey
of rising above and beyond
all that passed through her,
She is equipped with a knife of
contradictory saw-teeth,
Enabling her to cut
the weeds of duality,—
the breeders of pain,
Thus cleansing her path
to be a witness to all that there is,—
to be aware of the knowledge:
that all that is known
is unknown also at the same time.

And as she walks in her desert,
she flames through my being,
like some eternal presence,
to reach the oasis in my heart
for celestial lovemaking,
Drenched with the perspiration of love,
she walks even deeper into my heart,
making me a Sufi.

She is forever
walking nearer in(to) my heart,
while far away on earth she walks.

A little girl's love

O thou wonderful woman,
I'm honored
when you share
the innocent purity of a little girl's

wonderment about emotions
that you felt
in your near-puberty self for me,—
a grown up man at that time,
I'm honored to be the prism
through which you saw the
larger aspects of your womanhood.

It's like a tiny bud
sharing its story with
the sun, the moon, the dew,
the bees, the flowers and the spring air,—
all that which helped it in blooming.

Sainted wedlock

I'm a free spirit in my own way,
bearing my outer chains all intact,
Then you arrived
as the manifestation of
my free spirit
that knew the possibility
of free love and real freedom.

Your free spirit trapped in its freedom,
But freedom lay still and intact,
trapped within you,
And you proudly proclaim,
'So many freedoms are
enchained within me!
Aah, how much I'm trapped
in my set of freedoms!'

I see all this by holding you
as a mirror in my life,

This ecstatic insanity
makes me laugh and cry
without any walls between them,
And floating in that tranquility
I need not have your body
to feel you in me.

Exquisite intimacy

I'm feeling you in me,
For I'm never away,
Never really left,
Always watching you in me,
The tornadoes of your being
heave, dance and sing,
On your waves I'm surfing,
You too surfing on the
tidal waves in my heart
like a majestic queen,
All these ripples created by
the exciting uncertainty
of our undefined, free relationship.

You are all spirit
and float in air,
I'm all matter,
running on the ground
to catch your shadow,
You're the air that doesn't stop,
Holding your balance through
tantalizing misbalances,
But I'm a poet
and I can keep the shadows of air
in my heart like real things.

Your spirit has to
see the matter
as a milestone on your path,
While the matter has to
hold onto colorful dreams
to rise to a higher dimension.

A poet is a labyrinth,
Wherein,
only an unchained spirit like you
can dare to get in.

When I want you,
This itself is my fulfillment,
The distances melt
when I feel
how close you are,
Time stops
when I know here you are,
Right here in my heart.

Love's equation

Love is simply a natural need,
A pleasant sweet-sour greed,
It's as much the need to take
as is the need to give,—
the sizzling seesaw of give and take
that excitingly shake
our life's shape
and repackage it
with a new drape,
We have the need
to spread the seed
and fit in humanity's creed,

We have a need
to beat our fears
with bitter-sweet tears.

We are missing
many things in us
and we need those things
from that sweet someone,
Take it with a right
without judgmental blight,
We also need to give
something that we have,
Give without feeling as a donor,
This give-take is
above the feeling of indebtedness,
Giving here is equal to taking,—
An accounts equation
of the laws of soul,
Giving as good as taking,
We are joyful to give
and equally happy to take.
❁

Man and Superman

This planet, mother earth,
is one body,
When she is happy
the flowers bloom,
Ravaging floods are her tears,
Green pastures are her skin,
The verdant forests lungs,
Beautiful lagoons and lakes her eyes.

She is joyful, angry, kind,
cruel, healthy, sick,—

all these in her various parts,
Forest fires show her anger,
Spring dews on a rose show her joy,
Fruit-laden trees show her kindness,
Volcanoes catapult her seething anger,
She flaunts her health
in pristine rainforests,
She shows her sickness and famished body
through deserts and ribbed sand dunes.

It's a living entity,
Your very own Goddess mother
holding you on her palm,
Why seek godliness
far away in the cosmos?
It's right here around you,
in you, in her,
Sadly we can't see
what is already at home
and faraway we roam
looking for clues to divinity,
But all this while we just
walk away from it.

There is an imprint of godliness
in you, trees, ocean, flowers, snows, birds;
in everything,
Own it, accept it,
When we talk of seeking bigger truth,
we have a vision of the sum total
of our own tiny ones,
When we talk of godliness,
we mean our own humanness,
So stop, pause, rest, relax
and feel the super-reality
with your own super-self,
It's in you, around you, just nearby,

Worship this home deity,—
our very own mother earth,
You'll have paradise here only,
The unknown milestones of the afterlife
will blossom and manifest here only.

The Chief Butler

Caught in our kisses
and love-loops,
The ecstatic time
pays salutes!

Holy passage

Thus speaks the river
with its windy roar
and its rippling divinity all pure:

'There is a hole in my heart
that I offer you
as a passage
to move on your journey!'

The teachers

Sometimes the things
that would have come
naturally to you
as a human being
acquire a difficult shape
because they try
to make you learn these by force,
fearing you won't be

of any use without them.

In your natural state
you could have been useful,
at least like a plant that just grows,
giving its little share of oxygen, shade
and a little starter to some hungry goat.

But the attempt
surely kills your exclusivity,
Making you just a low-quality carbon copy
in a dog-eared folder.

The creator

At a given moment,
there is no absolute reality or truth or existence
beyond one's set of beliefs, knowledge, information,
set of conventions and collective mindset,
and the respective set of contradictions
of all the previous categories.

In our endeavors to find the absolute,
we simply shift
to a different set of all these categories,
We simply create a new plain of reality,
We keep pushing our truth
to cover more space
and adjust our ever-expanding desires and fears.

There is nothing to discover,
There is everything to create—
firstly, in ideas, imagination, emotions,
expectations, insecurity and fears;
secondly, its manifestation in physical reality
in the domains of art, science,

social conventions, economic models,—
everything.

Love

Sometimes you dump a person
even though she/he still has a bright smile,
twinkle in eyes and lovely fragrant words on lips,
Well, that's simply the sunset of love.

Sometimes you lovingly embrace a person
despite the frown, caustic remarks
and tightly pursed lips shut over bad odor even,
Well, that's simply the sunrise of love.

Love is simply a day
— or usually days at random —
in people's lives,
And that makes it
so ordinary, so natural, so normal,
Let it remain such,
Why make it otherworldly?

The naked hole

There is a hole in my heart
hanging like an ornate amulet,
And when sadness is groping
along the deepening twilight shadows,
it gets transfigured into a hook,
It sadistically pierces and
dredges the mud of memories,—
a perpetrator of pain,
It opens a gateway for

blatant intrusion of grief.

There is a craft of living,
To live is to look
hodge-podge normal on the surface,
So I express my grief and pain
through a laugh,
a casual remark and silly talk,
a smile, a joke,
a set of plain normalcy,
which help those around
in holding onto their concept of life.

The seasons change
but the springs and summers fail
to melt and thaw
the frozen heart
with its icy hole
leading to a cave
emanates from which a silent scream.

I know that
one has to learn to forget
to live and engage with
petty, chattering festivities
that sum up as
individual and collective life,
But the hole's hook is anchored deep
to keep the ship of my life
stranded in the betraying bay,
while the open sea beckons
with its waves and tides of freedom.

Look at love!
Its circuitous, meticulous forays,
It loops, tangles, untangles,
unites, breaks and finally shatters

the stones that were once pearls,
It has its gifts and allowances for the kids
playing to its script and direction:
some trace of truth in a lie;
some grain of lie in truth.

Slowly you get attuned to
this hole in you,
Still seeking love
you fall in love
with this missing chunk in you,
You hold the memories
in the pit of your soul,
And with the fire of your agony
and pressure of your grief
you crystallize them to diamonds,
Then you hold your self-mined treasure
and sadly muse over it
as the mystical emblem of all that
you missed, lost and grieve over,
You give it a precious title;
like we did with the golden earth
and named it as gold.

You get satiated,
You gloat and float
with air in you
that rushes through your hole,
You bob on the chance waves,
Your emptiness feeling like fullness,
You feel it has been worth it,
You stand like a gentleman
and proudly brace
the left pocket on your chest,
You put your hand on it,
You think you are looking victorious,
decorated, praiseworthy and well-clad,

But in reality,
you are simply
covering that naked hole in you.

In love with your place

One should know
how to fall in love with one's place,
It's an art, or rather craft
how to stamp and seal
the significance of little things,
little corners, tiny moments
and common people around you.

We just need an eye for them
and an open heart
to see, smell, touch, taste and hear
these soft, welcoming murmurs:
your very own neighborhood park,
local market street, corner shops,
the familiar people, the usual trees,
hoardings, banners, street dogs,
cats, cars, bikes, beggars, carts, vendors,
Everything that strikes you
with familiarity and recognition.

Some bench in a solitary corner
in the nearby park,
Some trees that look happy and healthy,
So also the ones appearing
sad, weak and brooding,
Some bird that you can recognize
among the rest of its species,
Some sound that you like—
be it a bird, animal or human,

Some hawkers that shout in your street,
The usual beggar that you see usually,
The brightest and naughtiest kids around,
Some beautiful smile on a lovely face
that makes you feel good,
Few people who wish you well on the way,
The old people going on their walks,
Someone's pet that fills you
with a good feeling,
The parked car that you would love to have,
The house that you like,
The paint that you like the most,
The dress on someone
that gives you positive vibes,
Someone's voice that is full of sweetness,
The chatty neighborhood grocer,
The busiest ones always hurrying,
The laziest feasting upon free time,
The oldest one going slow on the path of life,
The latest born with her rising sunrays,
The tree that looks sad and you empathize with,
The joyful tree,
The little backstreet lane
where you can walk,
The door that makes you feel curious,
The familiar and unknown faces.

Dear, your very own little place
has it all
that any other place possesses,
It's there,
Spot its pulse,
Accept its invitation,
Be its visiting guest
and go around like a joyful tourist,
And then it will spring so many surprises
to keep you entertained and relaxed.

Real love

Real love will be like water,—
flowing, cleansing, fresh,
It will softly brace you,
Give a very gentle touch,
It won't hit you,
It will be around you,
It won't try to barge into you,
It's there to keep you afloat,
not drown you,
If you drown that's due to your own
gasping fears and insecurities,
If you are open and give it space,
it will spread like a translucent sheet
as long as you have space in your heart,
where stars, sky, moon, clouds
will see how they look,
You will turn their mirror,
If you turn narrow like a gorge,
it will rush past with noise and fury,
It will rasp against your stony walls,—
not to break them
but to slowly make you realize
that these stony cliffs imprison you;
that actually these are what causes
this torrential roar in the flow of your life,
It shakes your precipitous slopes
to gently remind them the futility of
standing too rigid and haughty,
It doesn't try to attack or change you,
It just keeps with its gentle, wavy reminders
until one fine day
the steep slope of your rigidity melts

and falls into the stream by itself,
It doesn't try to push you out of its way
if the boulder of arrogance and conditioning
comes across its path,
It just flows past and around you,
Not leaving you alone
but always kissing your hard outer shell,
making you first mossy, round
and then you roll and flow
and settle on the painless bed of sand
it has prepared for you to rest.

That's real love,
It'll be always there
in one form or other
like water, vapor or snow,
It will save you from hate,
She may no longer
be the princess of your dreams,
or he your prince charming,
but you will still have enough reasons
to smile sometimes
far away in time and space.

An ode to the female athlete

Her soft, gentle, big eyes
full of hard, sharp determination,
Her long, supple limbs
flexible like a willow switch
full of steely, sparkling current,—
the current of life, beauty, resolve
carries the ineffaceable smile
under the stern, competitive mask,
She runs faster than

the divine feminine undulations
and exciting wavy fickleness,
She jumps higher and longer
than what the masculine eyes estimate,
She pushes, lifts, heaves, stretches
better than the man's expectations,
She is far more than
the weight of domestic routine in patriarchy,
She is a tigress, lioness, majestic queen,
She's the dancing *Shakti* on *Shiva's* head,
She is the thunderbolt
in a dark rumbling mass of cloud,
She's the spark of life in a stone,
She's the wind, the earth, the fire, the water
cascading in His *akash*.

Gain under the shades of pain

The lovely sadness of lost love,
a nostalgic shove,
a cooing dove,—
bitter-sweet, soft-hard love,
A soft-resigned moan,
Touching the spirit
that has this bodily loan,
The love that was
left behind as a milestone,
Now you walk alone
thinking of the days that once shone
with her presence sun like,
You are thirsty
but her memory is an oasis,
There you take shelter
from thirst, burning sands and storms,
There you cast away the weary rust

and the blinding dust,
There the fatigued caravan of life
drops its saddle,
And in the shade of that loving sadness
you feel better than
the concrete behemoths of comfort,
When you fall in love with you loss,
You can't be defeated anymore,
Nothing can redeem you
with its profiting gloss.

The beggar patient

In front of a hospital,
On the outskirts of a town,
On the starting point of a road divider,
Facing a crossing,
There she sits,—
a fragile, old, sickly woman,
Hunched and crouching,
A blanket and soiled bundle by her side.

There are dozens of patients in the hospital,
recovering, cared for,
They have money,
They have family and friends,
She but is all to herself
and some kind soul's mercy
who may stop, pause and give something,
Her head is hung low,
The eyes forever grounded,
She doesn't look at you;
doesn't say a begging word;
doesn't plead;
nor thanks you if you give something,

She is too poor and sick to give anything,
She hasn't even that much life
to even say 'thank you'
or give a little sad smile.

She is present
but life seems to be absent,
You can give some fruit or coins,
She is an open little box of misery
lying there to give you a chance
to feel kind and caring,
A wooden box almost,—
lifeless!
And a box doesn't speak.

Maybe some kind doctor or caring nurse
give her some pills sometimes
as their share in the domain of charity,
The beggar patient, they must be thinking,
Possibly she draws some security
by being so near to a hospital,
A mere look at the swanky, glass-fronted hospital
must be assuring her that she's at a hospital.

I have seen her a few times,
Sprouted like a mushroom on a dung heap
in the season of monsoon,
I also know she'll be gone suddenly some day,
But I'll remember the heavy presence
of her light body in her absence.

The destroyer of death

The thought, sight or proof of death
is disconcerting, mostly fearful,

But hold a dead butterfly in your hand
and death loses its meaning,
It looks so fragile, lovely, beautiful, colorful;
so near to life and all that it stands for
that the word 'death' loses meaning.

It feels a representative of eternal life,
immortally frozen in a moment,
Life's colors stamped with authority,
The form, the shape
dispelling the formless shades of death,
A colorful stamp of life
on the face of death.

The fearsome word loses its meaning
in association with a butterfly—
dead or alive,
The gist of smiles, fragrance, flying, nectar,
fluttering and playfulness,—
a life crystallized to a feathery diamond;
something bigger than even life,
Death looks so-so common in its face.

The pregnant woman

I can see that glow,
that joyous feminine flow,
I can feel that sense of fulfillment in you,
It's a smile not to win
but of sweetly losing to
the force of creation,
of which you are the carrier womb,
Serenity and acceptance seeping in you
as your stomach grows,
An acceptance of someone within you

to give it life
and nurture it with your own blood;
with love, smile and care,
Your eyes carry a deep contentment
despite all the pains and discomfort
you have to accept and welcome
to give a chance to a little life
to dance on the stage of creation,
You walk slowly and carefully;
the best steps you ever took;
each step measured and treasured,
You eat for her,
You feel for her,
You even avoid a tear for her sake,
You dream for her,
Your every cell is busy in its job for her,
Your slender, fabulous curves
melt under the heat of motherhood,
You joyfully abandon the prized and well-worked
standard statistics of your curvy figure,
Your bigger self is happy for her,
Slowly you change shape
and become a totally new person,—
for her, just for her,
You fly in your soul so that
she would be walking on her tiny feet,
You happily gain kilos
to give her a few extra grams,
You inhale happiness
so that she can feel its taste in you,
You walk through the tough field
of making a new life
with a selfless willingness,
This is the fulfillment in you
that you had been seeking for so long
while you stamped your caliber and authority
on the worldly stage,

You were exercising to take
the curve of your belly
to an inward feminine curvature
so that some day
you will let it loose
like a bow drawn tautly inwards
to unleash it with sweet, creative fury,—
the arrow of maternity,
The stomach drawn back with so much care
bursting forth with feminine force of creation,
There you launch your identity
to be a mother;
from a woman to be a mother,
A Goddess you look with your big belly,
Even lusty eyes have respect for you now
because you are carrying
a sacred baton of life now.

The death of a butterfly

A grounded butterfly
on the mossy brick floor,—
a flickering, flapping life
completing its last worldly chore,
A sad sight,
so many others flutter with delight,
suckling flowery smiles and nectar sweet,
Aha, life on full feisty treat,
And the sad, sick dying butterfly
with its wings shut tight,
jutted, sticking like one wing,
The air gone with the space between them,
A closing, a conclusion,
a finish to the chapter,
a final drop of anchor.

Just alive enough
to hold the wings tight and straight,
and a little movement of legs
to convince the gathering ants
that it's something alive,
imploring them to respect
the deathbed's sad sanctity.

A silent, slow parting from the world
in a rain-soaked mossy corner
in this big world full of
big-time meetings, unions and laughter,
She is deathbed, grave, cremation
right there in the centre of
throbbing life, raucous laughter and living.

Life still holding
like the vertical sail of a lost boat,
The ants sensing the death
which is their food,
But it has enough kick in its legs
to shake them off and move
for a little jog of life,
another tiny sip of survival.

The day progresses,
Time crawls slowly,
There is now a tilt in its
vertical lime-green sails,
With a slanted sail it moves,
Brave butterfly,
If you can't fly,
you should crawl,
Moving with shut-down slanted wings
is also the hallmark of life,
It shows that once you flew high,

The yard is now
an unknown grounded reality,
One more tiny step,
One more little sip of life.

It needs a flowery coffin, I think,
I hold the shut down wings
to take it to a cozy flowery corner
where it can die in peace,
But there is enough force in its wings
to give a tangible pull
to the fingers of a pitying poet,
It flutters to the core of its life reserves,
It denies the captivity even
in its last moments,
As I try to put it among the petals
of a lovely flower in a safe corner,
It denies the possibility of make-believe comfort,
It's brave; it loves its freedom,
It's even wiser than me,
Shakes to rebuff my denial of death,
It flaps vigorously, as if shouting,
'Let me be open and honest with my death
on the same old open, raw stage of life!'

It's no longer interested in flowers,
It has dropped its cravings for petals and nectar,
That was then, and now is now,
With marvelous detachment,
it uses her last ounce of strength,
swings and swirls and flops out of
the rosy bed I prepared,
'Flowers are for life;
ground is for death!' it seems to shout,
She makes this bold statement
with the last air in her wings,
almost gets airborne again

but lands on ground after
a few feet of painful, struggling flight.

It lands on the timeless bed of eternal sleep,—
mother earth,
It looks at me with a rebuke,
'What do flowers matter now?
They were for the time when
there was air and desire in the wings!'
And there she stands on the ground again,
strong, defiant, her sails vertical once more,
The antennae on alert
like a lacerated soldier still holding his shield
to parry off the last strokes of enemy swords,
Her legs dancing to accidental
bumps of the rushing ants,
Tightly holding the fort of life,
Seems to tell me,
'Give as much as you can,
as long as it's possible!'

She faces the end with dignity,
with calm deliberation,
with full alertness,
using all that is still left to her
to defend her identity of a butterfly,
And she does that with honor,
If not with flying colors
but with brave, straight sail
for almost four hours,
Then the vertical sail tips over,
Her little ounce of consciousness
seeks a way out,
The closed wings open
like the fists turning into the open palms
of a human dying and turning to a corpse,
She welcomes the skies

with open wings
and flies to subtler dimensions.

She is now a toy for the wind to play with
and food for the ants to enjoy,
Her colorful corpse flutters
and is dragged playfully by the wind,
The ants pursue the lemon-green food,
Its wings chipped like a cake getting cut,
Happy ants carry home the mementos of victory.

The butterfly is now air, sun, wind, sky
and water, fire, earth in the ants,
The little show of death on the ground,
The show of life in full abloom
among crimson clusters of peregrina flowers,
The corpse disintegrates on the ground,
While her sisters dance on the petals,
They suck nectar from flowery lips,
They flutter and play among leaves,
Dozens of them giving the best
a butterfly can give
in beauty, smiles, nectar and pollination,
Then silently one of them
comes aground like this one,
Floats like a dry, dead leaf
and gently touches the ground for eternal rest.

The show of many lives and smiles
and some deaths and tears,
Among happy flowers, waving leaves, floating clouds,
All under the eternal muse of that
who lives and dies side by side.

A real friend

The situation is 'as it is',
Thy knee under painful seize,
Humans may not be much support,
but look at the stick
taut with its supportive deport,
Listen to her lovely tapping song,
It is your extension for the time being,
A real friend
to see you through
to better days on a smoother path,
when the sun will smile
with brighter rays,
Happy, healthy all aglow
and walk of your own
with poise and steps slow,
Then one fine day
egged on by a sunny ray
it will find you strong again,
Sing it will then
a lovely farewell song
with its last tappings on your floor,
You'll then take up routine chore,
But don't forget your friend in need,
When there wasn't anyone
to pay you heed,
Don't throw it away,
Keep your friend in a corner
to remind you that
we are humans
and we need support,
We are here basically to *give*
but *receive* with grace as well.

Standing on the official tower of misery

On the far edge of pain
hanging over a precipice,—
where one loses all hope,
One step more
and it's all darkness,
Stand there on the edge,
Ponder over your choices,
To fall is the easiest one,
But isn't the easy choice
a trap laid by death itself?
Sometimes it's possible to go back
and walk into life's embrace.

Unswerving dedication to hope

From the musty corners
darkness can creep into one's mind,
Fight it if you will,
or you can.
If you can't manage,
let it come;
but at least don't allow it
to feed further on your hopes,
There will be a day
when the openness of clear sky,
freshness of forests,
brightness of sunrays,
smiles and smells of flowers
will also come rushing in,
Like crusaders to wipe away
the last traces of dark.

Classical beats of life

Lives crossing path
for a meaning,
Lives drifting apart,
Again for a meaning,
I suppose.

Bleached beings

Hate consumed love
and life's colors got bleached,
Dreams got washed away,
Smiles died,
Colorless people there are
despite all the external coloration of
fashion, make-up, design, vibrant exhibition,
and multi-colored thoroughfare.

Gratitude

How lucky I'm
even to stand amid my supposed
heap of miseries—on land,
It's a treasure because right now
someone is drowning—in water;
looking for a toehold
of land—dear earth,
It would be his treasure
just to stand on a garbage dump.

I might find this day drab and boring,
while someone would give all his wealth

to get another drab-most, boring-most day
—just a day.

How lucky I'm to live, breathe,
see, walk, touch, taste, feel,
while so many lose
their privilege to even these.

How lucky to have a home,
while so many go hunting
for a filthy corner
and put a plank, board, metal sheet,
lie under it
and call it home.

The clothes I wear,
the food I eat,
the people who love, care and smile at me;
even those who hate me
because they know me at least,
There are scores of those
who don't have any of these.

I'm rich and lucky in being alive,
I hold a treasure,
What makes me see it?
It's just 'plain old' gratitude,
The moment I lose it,
I lose everything,
Then I'm just a cribbing,
miserable, poor, suffering victim.

So my gratitude is my key
to the infinite luxury
and treasure I hold.

The grand illusion

Shifting shapes...
Fragmented forms...
Cracked creations...
Floating formations...
Transitory turns...
Brief beginnings, briefer ends...
A moment in the eternal NOW...
Visible clues to the invisible unity...

Evening Shades

Evening shades...
a musical silence...
a pleasant sadness...
a shifting stability...
a solitudinal companionship...
a sweet loneliness...
a whisper...
a dewy smile...
a place where light and dark have a date...

The old

The *Old*
doesn't want to leave its hold
against the *new* all fresh and bold.

An evening

If I look at it with my *mind*,
it is divided into pieces,
thoughts and feelings,
But the moment I don't mind the *mind*
the fragmented reality coalesces
to form a unified fabric.
Slowly rising moon,
Beautiful and amazing,
A glimpse of that most amazing unity,—
the celestial beauty.

She is going

She is going slowly,
looking back now and then
with her rosy smile.

To transform the dew drops
into shining pearls
by spreading the golden rays
of her youth
on some new horizon far away.

Perhaps to complete
whatever remained incomplete here,
To fulfill some unfulfilled dreams,
To brighten some dull eyes,
To bring a smile as sweet as honey
on some sad lips.

Go!
Trying to stop you would be like
blocking a new dimension of life,

Goodbye with a sweet and slightly sad smile,
Travel well and bloom profusely,
Bloom so much that your brightness
turns the dialectical pain of coming and going
redundant, irrelevant and meaningless.

From the mirror of the past

Today I looked into
the mirror of the past,—
a more than two decades old picture,
My 24-year-old self
smiled from behind the dust of decades,
And told me to keep living
with this peace
so that it (the old self)
can also see my reflection
in the future,
if someday it feels like
looking into the mirror of the future.

Moment to moment magnificence

The moment is frozen
but it breathes,
Slowly its stillness moves
and gently leaks into the air,
The eerie stalemate is broken.

Reality is just a
series of such moments,
Just like cinematography,—
a moving picture;

just snapshots of perception.

Vagrant virtues

Her smile
spreading into the sad air;
her laughter
a ripple in still waters;
her words
an assurance in chaos;
her touch
bringing life to a heart
that had turned into a rock.

A sad, soft and beautiful touch.

A succulent transparency in her whisper
bringing light into sorrow-swept eyes;
repairing a leaking heart,—
a check dam on the stream of pain.

Her soft but alert presence
filling the unfillable restless void.

Washed with her memory
here I stand,
Happy and sad
with all that is
good and bad.

Nature

Once the mind-noise stops,

it opens a door
to the deep melody of soul,—
mother nature,
which is the sum of
all the lesser sums.

The hunted hunter

We are less human
than we think
in our need of love,
We are nearer to the raw,
animalistic aspect of nature
as we go hunting our own needs,
which we present as
the selfless bouquet of love.

During our hunt
we carry oldest, pristine fears,
And like little animals
we seek safety
in the cave of love.

Freedom Vs Imprisonment

A part of me
lost touch with life,
A door was shut
upon a little alley of life,
Then I was blind to
that aspect of life
which the little alley carried
in its journey to the main street.

But whenever a door opens,
a part of your soul comes out
to mix with
a lovely piece of art, architecture,
pattern or design,—
man-made or
self-evolved
on the canvas of nature.

Spurting, seam-bursting sorrow

The night sky looks so close
and so big
from the top of this mountain,
I peer into it and read
the voluminous story of betrayal
written with splashy font
in her twinkling eyes.

Suppliant-stony & Bitter-sweet

Delicious flavor of freedom
lingering in her eyes,
The only way to taste it
was
through her lips,
Loving warmth tingled
in her body,
Giving a feeling of vast space
in her intense embrace.

Transfiguration

There is an indefinable nobility
and dignity in one's soul,—
the scented core of
one's essential being,
despite all the
muck, dirt and foul smell
on the surface,
Allow it to come
a bit closer to you,
Firstly in thoughts,
Reading can help you in this;
talking to nice people too;
opening the self in the unbounded
confession box of nature also,
Then slowly over a gentle
and slow period of time,
you can still bring it closer
to your seat,—
this body vessel,
You can bring it into action,
It then is like
holding a fragrant-most flower
in your hand,
And then you smile
in consonance with your soul.

Open treasures

Read the colors in a rainbow,
It's an open book,
See how the colors melt into each other
and make a pathway for dreams
across the endless cosmic streams.

Pick up a flower that has
happily dropped on mother's altar,
Smell it if it has fragrance to offer,
Marvel at its petals if not,
Or enjoy both if available in the bouquet.

Feel the friendly brace on your skin
by a leafy branch
as you rush past lost in thoughts,
It touches you to be present;
be *here* and *now*.

Soak the sunshine,
Feel its warming smile on you,
It showers you with warmth
to take you out of the frozen cave.

Feel the kiss of breeze
on the pores of your skin,
It absorbs your tension.

Walk with naked feet,
Mother earth will caress your soles,
Like sponge
she'll soak your agonies.

Feel the rain on you,
The drops will drum on your soul,
You'll hear its cleansing music.

Look into the open sky,
The formation of colors, shapes,—
the shifting canvas of eternity,
It'll teach you
to create without clinging.

Peer into the night sky;
into the galactic distances,
Receive the starry smiles and their sway
reaching you from millions of miles away.

Rich man, many treasures you own,
You just need to
acknowledge it with gratitude
without complaining groan.

A drop is the sea

A dole out
from the infinite unmanifest
to the finite manifest,
I am just a
tiny speck of cloudy phenomenon
casting its shadow in a little valley.

From the unbound infinity
to cosmos
to solar system
to Earth atmosphere
to this little fleeting shadow,
I am simply a ripple,
a pulsating craving,
a throbbing,
through which
the whole feels its own being!

Floating and flying

Life can be tricky,

if even about the simplest issues
you are too frisky,
Prudence is to be at ease
with situations and time,
Complications then wouldn't chime,
And days would pass like a free rhyme!

The traveler

We are not a mistake
to be corrected,
We are just humans
on our correct path;
just needing sometimes
kind, loving, caring words
from our fellow travelers.

A nostalgic tree

The sad musings of a lone pine
on a weather-beaten ridge:
Where have the birds gone?
Many of them used to roam
the sky over my head,
And play, love and make nest
at their joyous best
among branches mine,
Now my tree-soul doth pine,
Yesterday, I saw a bird couple too sad,
Are many of them dead?

The life song of a dead tree

My wood is all but dead and dry,
I oughtn't to have a sad tear in my eye,
Nor a pining heart's sigh,
My roots are now the soil
that fuels the fresh leaves' toil
for new smiles and fragrance,
Much of what was once above
is alive now below!

An Exit

The conveyor belt of pain
carrying the weighty stones of despair,
The bond of happiness dry and dead,
Soul aching with sorrow, anger, even guilt,
Body's cells colonized by fear,
Going alone and forlorn,
Feeling resentment against a world
where everyone seemed to have worked out
how to be successful and happy,
Everyone except himself.

Slowly receding from all possibilities of life,
Silently stepping into the pool of non-existence,
Taking a revenge against life
by retreating from its false promise,—
the lollipop of hope,
Presuming life had been repulsing him
by burning and charring his aspirations
not only of fame and grandeur,
but even the little things
that come naturally to everyone
whether they seek these or not.

His eyes like tall arched windows,
Face like a weather-beaten, mossy stone façade,
Body like an ancient battered brick structure,
A shattered star being sucked by a black hole,
Utterly frightened of life,
while all along he imagined
himself to be scared of death,
Haunted by the feeling of being incomplete,
Full of regrets for not being able to
welcome life as one should,
And that in a way
was an invitation to death.

Regrets constantly chiming in his chest,
The chances he squandered brimming his mind,
clouding him,
turning him blind to
the options and choices that had been beckoning,
trying to draw his attention.

Now, to forget the fear of life,
he decides to die.
A suicide.
A shameful exit.

Blinding the self

Mostly, we are viewing ourselves
in terms of what we are not
and what we couldn't become,
In this way,
we are simply repulsing life,
We deny our very own little reality,
our existence,

our life,
our twinkling little puddle
under the starlight,
We ignore the wild flowers
that offer consolation
if we give them a little bit
more than a cursory look.

Crowded loneliness

We are basically
a very lonely species,
Loneliness pervades our being,
Maybe we love being lonely,
And to keep its bitter-sweet charm,
we allow interruption to our loneliness
through love, affection, friendship, relationships,
But we know we have to
get back to be lonely again,
We are ready to pay the costs for it,
We squander away love and friendships
to buy our next installment of loneliness.

We carry the story of our loneliness
like a rock in our heart,
We treasure this dark piece,
We value it like gold,—
We bring a lighted interruption in between
just to realize and feel the extent
of this lonely darkness inside us.

The knight of life: love

A mysterious longing
smolders through the day
and burns at night,
An exciting anticipation,
An unsparing desire,
The pores of your skin
humming with excitement.

A feeling of remarkable audacity,
which makes you unbothered about
the usual jostle and hustle of life,
Something looks straight into your eyes,
And you flinch, get tamed and surrender
to a gleaming, flashy star.

Your sense of identity gets stable
in the chaos and hubbub of life,
You stand apart,
It even makes you feel proud,
even haughty,
to own this exclusive excitement,
You slyly smile,
A warmth spreads through you,
Melts the clods of uneasiness,
Overpowers your molecules of ego.

You flow,
You enter the season of spring,
A celebration begins,
Almost a rebirth and renewal,
You kiss the new sprouts,
You appreciate the flowers,

You feel the breeze on your skin,
Your eyes see the beauty around,
Your soul feels the all-pervading love
when your heart gets a sweet shove
at the mere look of your dearest dove.

Evolution at my cost

I would come closer by an inch
and you would step back by a mile,
An inch of reclaim
paid with a mile of declaim,
More inches breeding more miles,
You vanishing towards the horizon,
Then gone,
Then your memories would recede
in the same proportion and manner,
That's how time and space grow,
That's how this cosmos expands,—
at my cost.

The green leaf

Why be ashamed and apologetic
about what you are?
Why try to be
a fraction of your full self
to fit in the cast of others?
To gather fake sense of security,
it needs lots of explanation and effort,
By being a fraction of yourself,
you are like a fragile leaf on the ground,
lying there to be broken under others' boots,

But by being your full self,
you become a green leaf on a high branch,
soaking the sunrays,
kissing the dew,
and swaying to the free breeze.

The gardener

You left and I stayed
in the lovely orchard we'd built,
The garden, flowers, fruits and leaves,
where the soul now grieves,
Memories scattered around
like an autumnal drizzle of leaves,
And me like a gardener
hoeing, pruning, spading,
Working to bloom spring flowers in autumn,
Trying to undo the fall,—
the autumn that permanently
descended and sat upon the orchard,
Coloring it with yellow-brown colors of fall,—
Forever,
Toils where the gardener of springs
in an autumn-possessed orchard.

The backward flying arrow

The arrow of nostalgia
piercing through lost years,
Moving swiftly through cloudy past,
To hit home with precision,
To land at a moment,
A little dot in space-time fabric

containing a tiny slice of life
when we talked, held hands,
When just being together
was to feel full, rested, contended.

The storm-chaser

Love crushes you,
Consumes you,
It feasts upon you,
Dances on your head in wild revelry,
You become a stage
for its foot-tapping partying,
Its heels stomp on your chest,
Thump, Thump, Thump,
Your heart beats to its tunes,
Your soul sings to its composition,
Your eyes see its colors,
Your nose smells its fragrance,
Your fingers touch its curves,
Your tongue tastes its nectar.

It's almost like a possessing entity,
Something that descends upon you,
Shaping you at its whims and fancies,
It's not you,
It's above and beyond you,
You realize it when it drops its spell,
leaving you like a garden
lynched on a storm's path.

It's a tasty addiction,
You are deshaped and deflated
once it abandons you,
You then hanker after the same shape,

You become a storm-chaser,
You run after another storm
to be jostled, pushed, pulled, ruffled,
Hoping you will get a fresh shape,
you allow yourself
to be hammered on the anvil again.

Stormy addiction

It's a sea of all-consuming indulgence,
A vast, pleasure pool,
And like a little cork piece
you bob on its turbulent waves,
You get heaved, bashed, thrown in air,
You gasp for breath with excitement,
But storms can't last forever,
They have to stop and die,
Then you float lifelessly,
You pine for that high, that kick,
You feel life has drained out,
To be kicked by the storms of love
is what you view as being alive.

Songbird hunters

Autumn mist on a solitary trail,
A path leading into the woods,
Leaves dancing on your head,
The steps tuned to the rustling sound
like a child playing with fallen leaves,
Mother nature planting a sapling of silence
in the soil of solitude,
Joy melting from heaven

and falling on earth with each leaf-drop.

Here I walk,
Running away from the chained,
suffocating loneliness of a crowded bazaar,
Rushing and rustling into the
wild and free loneliness of this forest,
Crossing the intersection of bliss and torture
to enter the free domains of the former,
Exiting the shimmering and turbulent
zone of the latter.

But there are shadows here as well,
Here, where language is love and beauty,
Even here, the beautiful colors
and the songs of the songbirds
are chased by the curly tentacles
of the songbird hunter,—
the merchants of memories
who trap love and beauty
for worldly gain:
security, safety and convenience,
They lay the mist-net
to catch the present
in the invisible threads of the past.

A curator of freedom

Honey-dipped,
Dripping with grace and glee,
Almost a rain of sweetness,
Full of sadness and beauty,
This tiny grove dripping with
mystical indulgence and pleasure,
Shaping its own self

for a better world for others.

Here my frozen identity,
—curated with fear-born care—
starts twirling with a buzzing audacity
to dismantle the tiffin tiers
of honorific geometry,—
a tiny stack of food
for the little caged beast inside,
And throw it away
with a ballooning distaste
from the edge of the dark pit,
Meanwhile, cheers erupting
from the unchained soul.

Here just the smile of a flower
has the power
to turn one hopeful,
Here one need not hide oneself
in a corner
so that guilt won't reach,
Luminous streaks of some warmth
touch the chords of deepest sadness,
mellowing all arrogance and pretention,
pushing me out from the darkness within
where I'd disappeared
and couldn't find a way out.

What a great artist it is!
Stripping all falsehoods of their varnish,
Leaving them naked to the core.

Beyond the debate of
accidental or created change,
here the giddying fresh air
fills my lungs with freedom.

A moment of life in a dead lifetime

Fried, pickled and roasted by life,
And proud of the pearly beads
of hard labor earned on the skin,
We set out to seek freedom,
but end up getting more trapped,
Desperation dripping
from every pore of skin,
we die many times
in a single lifetime.

But even if we have lived fully,
in totality just once,
there shouldn't be any grudges,
Because this one moment of totality
is worth a lifetime of fractured being;
a moment of liberation
among the living chain of
restlessness and incompleteness.

This & That

Tell me a place where
light and dark don't coexist?
Or a heart where
good and bad don't struggle?
Tell me the land where
Gods exist without demons?
Or the sky where
heaven exists without hell?

A canvas of moss

In the mossy fluidity
of a solitary pool in a lonely vale,
I see my shadows
while the mountain breeze freely sail,
My spread self mixed with the mossy waters,
And I marvel
at the small canvas holding the image,
While the brook tries to rewrite the colors.

A stepping stone

Humans, you may have a stony heart,
But mine is definitely
a soft, mellifluous, mossy green one,
And I wear it on my sleeve,
While you step over my clean white yard,
And scamper away,
I just pray,
Safe you reach,
Without any further breach.

A slice of solitude

A slice of solitude,
Sometimes I own it myself;
sometimes I share it with someone,
Both means are important
in their own ways.

Carbon copies

We are like books,
Our appearance, identity, presentation
are like a book cover,
It's to attract
and be sold well,
The glittering cover and catchy title
to enhance valuation and price.

Unique covers to create curiosity
in the reader's mind and heart,
Showcased, we are then purchased,
But when the covers flip open,
pages unfold,
our lines read,
Alas, the story
that promised something different
turns out to be the same,
The same old, stale story,
written and phrased differently,
The same plot retold
with the same characters
named differently,
The same wine
in a different bottle.

The lean, loyalist hounds

The lion fattens itself
by eating the parts in others,
The net of fear, vanity, hate, jealousy
catches the prey,
He is the ruler,
The followers are the victims,—

the loyalists,
They get addicted to
the pleasure of self-laceration,
They cut down those parts of theirs
which annoy or displease him,
They allow the flesh
of their soul to be eaten,
They turn lean hounds themselves,
Grow sharp fangs of jingoism,
Get trim starved bellies,
Then they hunt themselves
to further fatten the king.

Miracle

The sun, moon, stars, dew, flowers, rivers,
It's a miracle unfolding every moment,
The thing that we call as a miracle
is just a tiny snap-shot of the Miracle,
Just a little framed reality
viewed in abstract;
delinked from the bigger chain;
put in a frame
and termed as a miracle,
But it's just a mere grain of salt
in the sea of the ultimate reality,
It's just human to try to
define the undefinable;
to try to know the unknowable,
The fact is, we just take a few drops of water
in our palm and see our stars in it
and call it a miracle,
But you are the miracle,
Everything and everyone is miraculous.

The kingdom of love

Falling in love
is like a magical rise,
The bored monotony of life
lies scattered on the ground,
Angels and fairies sing for you,
You're the prince of your airy kingdom,
But we can't float forever,
Earthbound we are,
That's life,
Falling from love is hard,
Becoming ordinary again is painful,
Losing the kingdom hurts,
Being a commoner again pinches,
Then we fight
to retake the kingdom,
Again we fall in love
and float.

It's unclear whether we're
more addicted to rise or fall.

Happiness

Happiness is like a meteor shower,
It hardly starts
before it ends,
But its brief sojourn
on the dark breast of the cosmos
is exciting, beautiful, sparkling—
the spark of life in a dead pool,
Like the verdant fresh look
on an old dusty face,—
the lush glimpse of hope, wisdom,

forgiveness and acceptance.

A small yet eternal book
without title and author name,
The lively flash of being
in the dark womb of nonbeing,
A smile on an impassive, sullen face,
A path-side wild flower
by a dusty path,
A brief shower on the sands
kissing the parched grains,
A warm hug,
A friendly chat,
Some words of empathy,
A smile,
That's what happiness is,
Brief and momentary,
but a yardstick for the eternity.

The hero

You've to be a bigger person
to say sorry first,
You've to be a strong person
to keep the imagined reality
shorter than the real one,
You need strength of character
to retain the worst for yourself
and pass the best to others,
You've to be a very brave person
to still smile even while shrouded in sorrow,
You need to be really living
to find a meaning in life
even with pain entwined in your soul.

The marks of sin

Some grains of wheat
turn to your morsel,
And maybe it was a bird, rabbit
or some other animal
that's on your feet
or head or on your legs
or torso,
Be watchful,
For you carry the sad marks of
transformation on your skin.

The pilgrim

Forlorn and friendless,
Heart fractured and ruptured,
Looking like someone
entirely made of grief and sorrow,
The dreams crumbling to dust,
Viewing this world
as an extension of my pain,
There I walk in the miserable rain
after having lain
in a dark corner almost slain.

Each step so heavy,—
like the dream
of a shadow to acquire a form,
Memories come with a roaring incision,
The wounded petals try to
furl the sail in the spring night air,
A step I must take,
Walk I must,
Because walking a single step

away from the garbage
is like a miles long pilgrimage.

The ceramic pot of memories

Silence louder than noise,
Her absence denser than her presence,
A flood of joyful pain
at her memories' touch.

My horde of memories
stored in a ceramic money-pot,
Storing her essence
drop by drop in the form of lovely coins,—
the colors of spring in her deep, big eyes;
the eyes the gateway to her soul;
the silken, straight tresses;
lips full with a pout of feminine mischief.

The ceramic pot of memories,
I hold it safe against a chance fall,
It's full, can't have more coins,
But I try to push one more coin,
Some new coin, glinting with
the polish of the present times,
But you can't recycle the rusted
coins of the past to mint new ones,
I want to keep the pot forever,
Because breaking it will scatter the coins,
And that would mean
losing even the illusion of still having her,
So the dilemma to keep it or break it
works like a see-saw cutting the heart's meat.

The demonic holy-book

A book,—
my scripture,
Having a love note
and a rose
slipped between the pages,
I don't open the page
where the love note stays safe
because opening it might
tear it at the folding edges,
I don't open the page
where the dry rose lies in its grave
because it will fall apart if touched,
Is it a holy scripture
or a demonic book?
For I love it so much
as to get scared to touch it.

The sweet slayer

Her presence in my life
dissolved and crumbled
like a sand castle on a beach,
I think love
—with some dodgy warmth about Her—
is always seeking a human way
to first maim and then kill you,
She seeks a suitable way
to slaughter you with a sweet smile,
while you feel your entire self
has become love,
To dump you into the pits
while you ride the cusp of Her wave.

The solitary trail

Deeply inhaling
the giddying fresh air of life,
The shower of peace
diluting all guilt and sorrow,
Slurping on the luscious slice of solitude,
Feeling the ease of life's movement,
Safe and secluded
from the snooping spies of life,
Away from squeaking chaos and gawkish glory,
I walk on this solitary trail
in almost absolute freedom,
It's such a beautiful sketch, this place,
Drawn with a child's coloring pencil,
As of *Now*, I own this little world
with composure and comfort.

Make hay while the sun shines

Hot and dizzy with love,
Flooded with joy,
Running into the flames of passion
to dance in the fire of love,
Go fella go!
Grab your hard-won moments of love
fleeting before the storm of hate,
Enjoy it to the core
while you are at love's peak.

The winner

All gaudy and grandiose,

Tightly hemmed with haughtiness,
Stepping up the curved staircase
leading to lustrous halls,
Thick-skinned crocodile
equally tempered in
harangues and soirees of life,—
the same demon walloping in mud for mating
and among the flesh of caught prey.

Even before he feels it,
guilt morphs into shame,
which is quickly covered with anger,
And anger has been
the driving force of his success,
The success as we know it and applaud it.

He has lost just little to gain much,
Just a tiny loss:
He's lost the touch of life in his eyes,
His glassy eyes are no longer
capable of expressing love,
That's the only little loss,
A loss at all,
if you think it to be.

Shared bestiality

The roaring chaos
churning the individual identities,
Meshing them
to make a peculiar fluid.
Then the deshaped mass
finding a strange rhythm;
coalescing into a weird shape.
An indefinable mass.

An uncontrolled animal
thundering with a collective roar.
The mob.
The crowd.
The rampage.

The ghost hunter

A strand of
the scent of jasmine
on dark night's breath,
It enters the crack
in a concrete heart,
It bores a tunnel
through the stony mass of pain,
To reach the core where
the ache has perpetually lain;
to be as near to it as possible;
to melt into its heart;
to become pain itself;
to transform its soul,—
its fundamental suffering self.

The strand of fragrance
with determination on the tip of its wings,
Chasing the ghosts of pain
meandering like a serpent,
To possess them;
hunt and haunt them;
get them embodied with love;
convert them into the religion of hope.

The hunter of sunrays

The hungry hole
in the soul,
Gobbling the light
to feed its darkness,
And when the sun
is at its noontime peak,
I peep into its depth
and watch the feeble slivers of light
rippling like some paranormal fish,—
predatory darkness
eating the slivers of light
like an eternally hungry dark shark
clawing at the sunrays.

The frozen waterfall

A frozen waterfall,
Its flow coagulated and coalesced,
A bluish white suspended corpse,
Bearing its beady threads of eerie stillness,
Both scary and beautiful.

A frozen flow,
Mummified tiny streams,
Caught and imprisoned
in the deep chambers of icy winters.

A hanging frozen life,
A dangling grave,
Icy ripples, folds, noodles,
paranormal braids,
crooked translucent curls,—
cold, lifeless, glassy.

A tangled hibernating mass,
Waiting for the spring sun
to dissolve and melt
and get liberated from the entrapment;
to gush out from the frozen womb of silence;
to chime with rippling songs of life;
to cascade with pride and vanity;
to get back to the business of life;
to flow with the song of spring;
to unleash its frozen soul
with flowing, falling, rippling warmth.

Locked and sealed

The heart that once was
an open meadow
adorned with wild flowers
is now a forlorn, fenced yard,
Its bosom sealed with pavement slabs,
Through cracks in these,
a few grass sprouts raise their head
in memory of better times:
free pastures, wild flowers, holding hands,
an embrace, a gentle kiss and a promise,
All that is now sealed under the slabs
and squeezed tight by the fence,
The few tufts of grass
sullen and somber like a grave's cover,
entombing a life that once was.

That love and its beauty is buried now,
The few strands of grass
peeping through the pavement cracks
hark like ghosts from distant past,

while the present's heels
go crushing over them
busy in profiteering deals.

The unseen foundations of success

The stories of a few winners
stand on the foundations of
the stories of millions of losers,
The stories of the winners
are meaningless and incomplete
without the stories of the losers,
Because what will the chief protagonists do
without scores of minor characters,
They are the unknown, busy ants
pulling the long lines of food for the queen,
The side players;
the little threads
that hold the plot together,
What worth a winner holds
without scores of losers?
What value light possesses
without the pools of darkness around?

A sad stream and a sullen heart

A bubbling creek
rippling with a miasma of pain,
A twinkling ribbon of solace
to a sad heart
as it ponders on its bank.

Does it—the brook—have the ability

to smell sadness in others?
And offer its own song of pain
as the musical chimes of joy to the visitor.

A flowing sadness and a frozen one,
Both of them turning friendly
to withstand the shower
of the frozen pellets of pain.

Friction

A frictionless life
is no existence,
Because without the rub of pain
was there ever any gain?
The stress, the tension, the pull, the push
keep us touching life's surface,
They are the agents of survival
guarding us against doom and decay.

The friction between
our dreams and the reality we face;
between what we fight for
and the result we get;
between smiles and bitter tears;
between love and hate;
between giving and taking;
between dark and light.

This friction is what
keeps the chariot's wheel moving,
This rub between joy and sorrow
creates the spark,—
the spark of life,
This grazing between

what is and what we desire
fuels the palpitation of life
in the tiny point of our existence,
It propels this little heartbeat
in the bosom of vast cosmos.

This friction is our causal force,
No point in hating it,
Come to terms with it,
It's like accepting the grounding gravity
without which flying is meaningless.

The frozen world

Holding your memories
is like embracing a pillar of ice,
It won't melt,
Rather the holder's flesh will freeze,
The iciness with a mysterious code
where one gets sucked
into its voluptuous embrace.

Walking with your memories
is like passing through a kind of
lavender-scented glacial landscape,
Driven into a scented icy mirage,
Where the heart gets frozen
with pain entangled in it,
A frozen heart inside a frozen persona
in a frozen landscape,
And life and living
shrinking into invisibility.

Me frozen here
and you flowing there,

An ice wall
separating our different worlds,
The storm of pain
now freezing and settling into
a dull, persistent ache
in a frozen heart.

The eraser

I'm in enchanting fascination with life
when you melt to joy in my embrace,
Pleasure swimming on the wings of
freedom in my rushing blood,
Joyfully the sun setting around me,
The light in your eyes
dwarfing the looming darkness around,
Your touch crafting a sweet tenderness,
Excitement pulsing through
our shared identity,
The expansive sweeps of time
narrowed to the tiny
curve of your lips.

Now when the fairy lights are off
and transitory rewards gone,
If an eraser must be
for all those moments,
let it be a soft one,
not hard like wire bristles,
I hope
that's not asking much.

The war

Some fighting
to douse fire in the belly,
Some in the mind,
Some in the heart,
Some in the soul,
All fighting for food, knowledge, love,
And these sire a concoction of ambition
to breed
anger, fear, insecurity and greed.

The killer kindness

Sometimes
pitying eyes
hurt more than
hateful
and angry words.

Not yet ready

Soiled with shame,
Scratching the crust of grief
on the skin
to make it a live wound,
most of us are not yet
ready to heal;
just not in acceptance
of the idea of healing and wellness.

The warrior woman

By giving your hate, lust, greed to me,
you can't change, redefine, transform,
or undo what is essentially me.

The shower of your scorn off balances me,
That's natural,
But I'm not a product of
what you do,
Yes, the bushfire of your lust
burns my luxuriant canopy,
But there are seeds under the ashes,—
the carriers of my legacy;
the seeded me;
the tiny container of my fundamental code.

It just takes some time
for the rains to wash away the ashes;
for the sun to kiss infant saplings,—
the little me pampered by mother nature,
And the small me will be a full me some day.
I'm inching closer to that reality
from the nightmare you've held me in;
from the prison of self-loath, anger, helplessness
to the beautiful grove of love and light.

The hidden hole

All of us have one primal need,
An emptiness, a deep desire,
A hole in the soul
that works as the core of our existence,
It fuels the impulse to live and exist,
It shapes our body, thoughts, emotions

like a pot maker
shapes wet earth on his wheel,
We spin to its force,
We bend, curve, mold
to the expertise of its hands,
This want or need is crystallized
with clarity in our soul's pit,
Buried and hidden under
a thick, black cloak of confusion,
But below the rubble of what others see
this is the most real thing about us to *be*.

The subsurface chaos

We believe we know a person
till some happening
finds us staring at a stranger,
All familiarity gone,
Because it's hard to have a sense of
the vast expanses of the unknown
hidden inside a person.

You may have heard a million words
from a mouth,
but we are also full of
trillions of unspoken words,
You may have seen tons of smiles
on a charming face,
but these hide rivers of tears as well,
You are acquainted with love
but it swims like a thin layer of oil
on deep waters of hate and pain.

Beyond the familiar stale stimulation of
superfluous comfort,

there is a stealthy man-whore
prowling in the shadows of love,
Beyond the lovely musical whispers
emanating from beautiful lips,
maybe there is a scream
imprisoned in the curvy lithe body;
vibrating inside,
looking for a way out.

As you play at the level of body,
don't forget the pain locked inside the soul,—
the epicenter ready to unleash earthquake
upon the outer shell,
Because below the apparent stable crust
there are thrusting, shifting plates.

The chasers

Sometimes even forgiveness
falls short of
accepting the reality,
Sometimes even love
falls short of
accepting the truth,
Sometimes even kindness
falls short of
looking over the hurt,
Sometimes even gratitude
falls short of
accepting the joy of what we have.

We are after all mere shadows
chasing the forms that we dream about.

Blindness

Everyone is
beautiful, pretty, handsome,
gorgeous, attractive, exquisite,
magnificent, brilliant, bewitching, dazzling,
enticing, alluring, graceful,
divine, delightful, elegant,
captivating, fascinating, sublime,
charming, glamorous, aesthetic
in his/her own way.

The spots of dislike
that we see on them
aren't actually
the dark markings on them,
These are the spots
on the retina of our own being,
preventing, obstructing full vision,
Making us partially or completely blind
to the beauty around.

Clean the eyes of your existence,
Then all you see is just
beauty, love and grace.

The endless stream of pain

Serrated with the pain of survival,
a man cuts a tree,
Resin and sap oozing from
the cut on the tree's bark,—
coagulated tears,
It's a tiny stream of pain
that started in a human heart

and changed to the tree's tears,
The stream of pain proceeds further,
It now becomes
the sad words of a poet
on the paper made of the tree's flesh,
The sad verse then chimes
with the inaudible whisper of pain
in some reader's heart.

The pack mule

Sometimes apparent luck
is leading us into bad luck
further on the way.
Then you realize you have
a mountainously bulky foolishness
inside your little shallow brain.

Out of the whirlpool

The more he came to know,
the more he realized
how little he knew her,
It was all there to see now,
Her pointless rambling pride,
Concisely pointed narcissism,
Habitually despondent demeanor,
Her efficient effrontery,
Swift certain selfishness,
Extensively ornamented body
covering a poor soul,
Her manners laced with

coquetries and jealousies,
All this he saw now.

Earlier, the whirlpool's vortex
sucking, pulling him into
soft languor and pleasure swoons,
Shaken, swirled by the eddying currents
now he got spewed out of
the vortex's pointed base,
Gasping for breath,
he came to the surface
from the edifying depths,
Looked at her with a
frigidly disagreeing look on his face.

Falling out of love is perhaps
just to know more about a person,
Maybe we are addicted to the fall,
And fly just for its sake,
Because, however high a kite flies,
it still survives by constantly eyeing earth,
Maybe love also flies
to enjoy its habitual crash-landing.

Metallic maggots

Mother earth says:
'O ye children, give me all your blood,
gore, filth, garbage, poison, chemicals,
I'd still give you flowers, trees, pastures.'

A mother can't stop giving,
She has to keep giving,
Till her last breath,
Till she perishes.

When the last flower on earth will die
along with the mother's last breath's sigh,
Her children would then
be replaced by a new species,—
the humanoid machines
that'll infest her rotten corpse,
It'll be a global grave
swarming with metallic maggots.

The guest

A drooping branch,
hanging with juicy glee,
bearing a ripe fruit.

It's in fact a tree's invitation
to a guest to its house,
'Come, taste some!' it waves,
Accept the hospitality,
Be a well-behaved guest,
Enjoy the delicacy,
And reciprocate
by treating a tree well
when it needs your help.

The true pearl

A fragile world we set up
around ourselves with our dreams,
destinations, envy, hope and fears,
Then we create a shell of hate
to keep the pearl of love in it,

It glitters,
But it isn't a love-gem,
It's our hate crystallized for self-deception.

Love comes with the inclusion of
more and more around you into your care,
And in this fertile soil
blooms a flower,—
love for someone.

Rain in vain

A hardness building up
in the soft, mushy zone
that enveloped us,
And the night even though
aglow with fireflies
lost its charm
like candles going off
when hit by
a howling blizzard.

She was silent outside
but screaming inside,
Crispy above
but pain-roasted below,
Flitting, flirting and dancing on surface,
but weary and bedraggled inside,
There we were
forcing ourselves to assume that
things were normal, even though
there were many proofs to the contrary.

There we were
pushing each other

into the pools of pain,
Earlier it was a
joyous jaunt in the rain,
Aah, the rose that blossomed in vain!

Miserable by default

Very rarely and very few
get finally really settled,
We are forever migrating,
We are a jumpy species,
Never on solid earth,
It seems the only inheritable things are
pain, sorrow and suffering,
But joy and happiness
we have to create in this very life,
Nurture as a dream, a destination
as we move on the
default mode of misery.

A suitable time

It was the time to
unlock the fears lodged in my guts,
and get in step with the chaos of life;
to take slander, gossip and mockery
as relevant and lofty as the scriptures.

It was the time to
take it as success to be heaved
and propelled by the current of pain.

It was the time to

take chipped, chaffed, moth-eaten humanity
as the post-modern goddess,
and worship her
while wearing clean clothes outside
and a filthy mind and heart inside.

It was the time to
be like everyone around,
And be a hunting hound
devouring the rabbits soft
and stay in the highest loft.

It was the time to
keep cupping the ears
to avoid any chance pick-up of
the upbeat melody of life,
And get used to the strife.

The book of silence

A little sad smile
that briefly dispelled the dark
like a lamp does with enlightening hark,
Then it vanished,
But in that brief light,
he read the book of pain in her eyes
written in a strange language.

It was just that little smile
that connected him with the stranger,
There wasn't anything to say,
It wasn't required in fact.

The rainbow in a stormed sky

Brave and foolish youth,
The sun-baked verdancy of curiosity,
The moth, the flame, the burning,
The rain of passion,
A riotous blizzard of emotions,
But the storms die,
The clouds get empty in the sky,
The skies clear,
Leaving a brief rainbow behind.

Love is a little arc,
a tiny rainbow,
It's drawn between two points:
joy and ecstasy at one;
pain and tragedy at the other.

Sandeep Dahiya

Sandeep Dahiya, fondly known as "Sufi," is a multifaceted Indian author, writer, poet, novelist, essayist, and blogger whose literary voice resonates with profound poetic reflections, empathy, love, and an unwavering celebration of humanity. Hailing from a Haryanvi village in Sonipat, and shaped by the contrasting vibrancy of Delhi, Dahiya's works bridge rustic traditions and modern sensibilities. With over 20 books to his credit, spanning fiction, non-fiction, creative non-fiction, and poetry, he has carved a niche as a literary virtuoso. Titles like Faceless Gods, A Half House, Mists on the Moon, Runaway Husbands, Beyond and Beneath, The Shape of My Love, The Notebook of a Nobody, The Notebook of a Self-unmade man, The Notebook of Dancing Shadows, and Love: The Ultimate Alchemy showcase his ability to weave intricate tales that delve into the human spirit.

Sufi's blogs, *Desi Blooms* and *Musings and Mutterings*, offer a glimpse into his unique style—intimate, reflective, and rich with metaphors. His writings, often set against the backdrop of rural India, explore the extraordinary within the ordinary, portraying common people as unsung heroes navigating life's complexities. A triple postgraduate in English Literature, Journalism, and Ecology, and with a decade of editorial experience, Sandeep infuses his narratives with intellectual depth and lyrical grace. His works transcend genres, blending spiritual musings with social commentary, as seen in his poignant essays and tender poetry. Based in the north Indian countryside, Sufi's pen continues to illuminate the beauty of existence, making him a cherished voice in contemporary literature.

Sufi's writing is marked by an emotional depth that resonates with readers, offering insight into the human experience and exploring the complexities of the heart and mind. His unique style blends introspection with a profound sense of connection to the world around him. Whether meditating on the nuances of daily life or reflecting on universal themes of love and longing, Sandeep's writing captures the essence of human emotions with grace and sensitivity.

Through his words, Sufi not only entertains but also enlightens, fostering a deeper understanding of the world and the people within it. His literary journey continues to inspire and touch the hearts of readers across the globe, solidifying his place as a distinctive and influential voice in modern literature.